Dream Guidance

Interpret Your Dreams and Create the Life You Desire

2nd Edition

Anna-Karin Björklund, M.A.

ARS METAPHYSICA

an imprint of Sunbury Press, Inc.
Mechanicsburg, PA USA

an imprint of Sunbury Press, Inc.
Mechanicsburg, PA USA

Copyright © 2012, 2021 by Anna-Karin Björklund.
Cover Copyright © 2021 by Sunbury Press, Inc.

Sunbury Press supports copyright. Copyright fuels creativity, encourages diverse voices, promotes free speech, and creates a vibrant culture. Thank you for buying an authorized edition of this book and for complying with copyright laws. Except for the quotation of short passages for the purpose of criticism and review, no part of this publication may be reproduced, scanned, or distributed in any form without permission. You are supporting writers and allowing Sunbury Press to continue to publish books for every reader. For information contact Sunbury Press, Inc., Subsidiary Rights Dept., PO Box 548, Boiling Springs, PA 17007 USA or legal@sunburypress.com.

For information about special discounts for bulk purchases, please contact Sunbury Press Orders Dept. at (855) 338-8359 or orders@sunburypress.com.

To request one of our authors for speaking engagements or book signings, please contact Sunbury Press Publicity Dept. at publicity@sunburypress.com.

SECOND ARS METAPHYSICA EDITION: May 2021

Set in Adobe Garamond | Interior design by Crystal Devine | Cover by Lawrence Knorr | Edited by Lawrence Knorr.

Publisher's Cataloging-in-Publication Data
Names: Björklund, Anna-Karin, author.
Title: Dream guidance : interpret your dreams and create the life you desire / Anna-Karin Björklund.
Description: Second trade paperback edition. | Mechanicsburg, PA : Ars Metaphysica, 2021.
Summary: This illuminating and practical how-to-guide gently guides you through the steps of lovingly connecting with your dreams and embracing your inner wisdom and intuition. Full of rich inspiration, dreamy teachings, and soul guidance, Dream Guidance 2nd edition invites you to embark on an inner journey of soul transformation and dream fulfillment
Identifiers: ISBN : 978-1-62006-557-0 (softcover).
Subjects: BODY, MIND & SPIRIT / Dreams | BODY, MIND, & SPIRIT / Inspiration & Personal Growth | SELF-HELP / Dreams.

Product of the United States of America
0 1 1 2 3 5 8 13 21 34 55

Continue the Enlightenment!

Disclaimer: No part of this book is intended to substitute for competent medical diagnosis or professional psychological services.

To all dreamers around the world.

Contents

Preface to the Second Edition	vii
Acknowledgments	ix
Introduction	1

CHAPTERS

1	Jungian Dream Psychology	9
2	Dream Characters	16
3	Dream Connection: A Step-by-Step Guide	22
4	Dreamy Intentions	39
5	Messages from Your Nightmares	49
6	Synchronicity: Guidance is all Around You	55
7	Intuitive Dreams	62
8	Dream Themes	68
9	Dreaming of Numbers	91
10	Dreamy Miracles	103

Bibliographical Notes	112
About the Author	115

Preface to the Second Edition

Warmest welcome to the new edition of *Dream Guidance: Interpret your dreams and create the life you desire*. I invite you to join me on an illuminating journey into dream realms, where we will embrace the fine nature of dreams and open the portal to soul growth and dream fulfillment. Since the publication of the first edition of this book, almost a decade ago, my appreciation for the guidance that is revealed to us in our dreams has only deepened. My love for dream creation and soul dreaming has only magnified, and I have had the deep honor of working with many beautiful dreamers around the world. I have also joyously been exploring the significance of numbers in our dreams, an endeavor that was originally inspired by Carl Jung's fascination with numbers.[1] Over the years, my sacred connection with numbers has only deepened, and I am very honored to include a chapter about the significance of number dreams in this second edition of Dream Guidance. The language of the Universe is composed of numbers and symbols, and each number vibrates with a unique frequency and carries a vibrational meaning. The messages that come to us through numbers in our dreams continue to mesmerize me.

In this new edition, you will also find that some chapters have been caressed with a loving touch, and some sections have been expanded to include more dream examples. Writing books is my highest calling, and returning to my first work to create a second edition has been a true soul honor. I very much hope you will find the new edition inspiring, illuminating, and enriching on your path of soul growth and dream fulfillment.

With Love and Gratitude,

Anna-Karin Björklund

Acknowledgments

The new edition of *Dream Guidance* may not have existed had it not been for the wondrous invitation I received from Steve Harvey to appear on his fun daytime TV show on NBC. Thank you Steve with all my heart for giving me the opportunity to share my love for dreams on your enchanting show, and for so graciously shining so much love and light on my book.

I would also love to express my sincerest gratitude to the International Association for the Study of Dreams (IASD). Since joining IASD in 2011, I have been blessed with so many deep soul connections, and I have found a community that now lives in my heart. I am very grateful, honored, and humbled to have served IASD as Chair of the Board over the last two years. This is a role I have truly cherished with my whole heart and soul. I would like to thank all members and board directors of IASD, and a special token of gratitude goes out to Scott Sparrow PhD, Laurel Clark D.D, Clare Johnson, PhD, David Kahn, PhD, Rita H. Hildebrandt, Angel Morgan PhD, Michelle

Carr PhD, Robert Waggoner, Jean Campbell M.A, Bob Hoss M.S, Julie Sparrow, Bob Krumhansl, Kimberly Mascaro, PhD, Linda Mastrangelo, M.A, and Bambi Corso for the special role you have each played in my life while rewriting this manuscript. It is an honor to walk on the path of dreams and soul growth with you.

    I would love to thank my mom and my dad and my whole family for your infinite love and compassion. Thank you also to all my friends around the world for your heart-warming presence and encouragement through all my endeavors. Most of all, I would like to thank my beloved daughter Angelina – you inspire me every day to live with an open heart and flow through life in joy and gratitude. Thank you so much for being you!

Introduction

Dreams are wonderful in so many ways. They not only help clear unconscious emotional blockages and enhance our awareness but miraculously also guide us with beautiful messages, premonitions, and unique wisdom. During our nightly dream voyages, the adventures we embark on can feel as real as events out of an ordinary day or as remote and foreign as though we were in a different time and place altogether. Some dreams help us with just the right guidance needed at a particular point in time. Other dreams help us foresee events in the future that we could never have predicted in waking life, or we may even dream about an event happening simultaneously in another part of the world. Yet we are still inside our mind the whole time . . . or are we?

Even though most of our dreams relate to our personal circumstances, we sometimes dream about life issues, situations, people, or maybe even places or dimensions we have never heard about. Or we get urgent premonitions that don't relate to our own lives in any way. If we were truly inside our own minds the whole night, how could we possibly receive all this information? According to the late Swiss psychiatrist Carl Jung, when we dream, we tap into the collective unconscious.[1] Jung described the collective unconscious as a shared field that connects us all, even beyond the limits of time and space. This field can also be likened to the notion of an astral plane or the Eastern understanding of an underlying Tao.

Even if you don't always remember your dreams, you can probably think of at least a few occasions when you woke up and couldn't help but wonder why you just had such a strange dream. We often draw on material from the astral plane or the collective unconscious to help make sense of our own lives, and sometimes we even reach insights that stretch our understanding of the whole Universe.

As a lifelong dreamer and devoted dream worker, I have studied the theories of many inspiring dream teachers, magnificent dream researchers, and spiritual teachers around the world. One thing that I have found through my extensive research, analysis of other people's dreams, and, last but not least, from my nightly journeys into the dream realms is that we may never know exactly what a dream is trying to tell us, or what it means. Dreams are highly complex and filled with multi-dimensional interpretation possibilities. Most importantly, all dreams are not meant to be analyzed or interpreted. The best way to work with some dreams is to experience them and connect with them on a deep soul level.

Introduction

In contrast to the more generic dream books and dictionaries often seen on bookstore shelves, the dream connection examples and dream interpretations in this book emphasize the importance of personal feelings, associations, and dream context, while also inviting intuitive guidance and sacred connections. You will learn how to categorize the type of dream you had and see how you can work with any type of dream by following an easy step-by-step approach and asking specific questions (see chapters 3 and 8).

THOUSANDS OF YEARS OF DREAMS AND INSPIRATION

The interest in dreams is by no means new. There is documentation of dreams reaching back thousands of years. In ancient Greece, they had dream temples dedicated to dream healing and receiving sacred messages from the gods. Native Americans placed high value on their dreams as well. Some Iroquois tribes even believed a person could get very sick if dreams were ignored.[2] As we will see in the chapter about nightmares, the Iroquois were right about the importance of dreams. If we ignore our dreams, emotional blockages are built up, and we do indeed risk becoming sick. Many world religions also honor dreams. Many sacred dream revelations can be found in the bible. In his book, *Dreaming in the World's Religions*, Kelly Bulkeley discusses how early Christianity viewed dreams as a means of communion from God to humans.[3]

DREAM GUIDANCE

In Buddhism, Tibetan practitioners of Dream Yoga view dreams and sleep as a monumental time for enhancing our awareness. Careful attention is therefore placed on going to bed with a clear state of consciousness. For more information about Dream Yoga, I recommend checking out the beautiful work by Tenzin Wangyal Rinpoche.[4]

Within the Australian Aboriginal culture, there is the concept of "Dreamtime," the space where everything is created and dreamed. According to this tradition, we dream ourselves into this world and then back into Dreamtime. The Australian Aborigines' view on dreams illustrates that there is, in fact, no differentiation between past, present, and future. It is all happening in Dreamtime. In the chapters about synchronicity and guidance, we will see that we can miraculously dream about something that is simultaneously happening in another part of the world or dream of a person we haven't seen in years, only for them to show up on our doorstep the next day. The concepts of time and space may not be as fixed as we believe them to be.

Many scientists and fiction authors have also drawn inspiration from their dreams. For instance, author Robert Louis Stevenson dreamed up the story of Dr. Jekyll and Mr. Hyde, and the Russian chemist Dmitri Mendeleev received help from his dreams when he discovered the right order of the elements according to their atomic weight.[5]

DREAMS AND PSYCHOLOGY

Both Sigmund Freud and Carl Jung integrated dream analysis into their analytical work with clients and saw

Introduction

dreams as a vital component of psychological growth and health. Jung's contributions to dream psychology came to be even more encompassing than Freud's, and he developed a broader spiritual understanding of dreams and the connectedness between us all. Jung's dream concepts have been integrated into many of today's psychological theories and form the backbone of many teachings in the field of personal growth.

I value dreams from both an emotional well-being and a spiritual growth perspective in my work with clients. We spend about a third of our lives sleeping, and perhaps as much as half of our lives in half-conscious states. As dreams flow from our unconscious, they can reveal many hidden aspects of our personalities and life situations that we are not yet aware of. Therefore, if we were to just look at what we think we are experiencing in our daily lives but ignore what is happening in our dreams, we would miss out on highly valuable information. By listening to our dreams, we integrate all aspects of ourselves and form a more complete picture.

It is also important to remember that our egos represent only a small component of our total selves. Consequently, our ego will always have just a partial view of life because of limited consciousness, so the importance of embracing our dreams cannot be emphasized enough. By looking closer at your dreams, you not only learn more about what is going on in your life, but you also develop new attitudes and perspectives on situations. You may, for example, not be aware of feeling upset about something, but then a dream helps shed light on the issue. Instead of forming an emotional blockage, you can clear it out by processing the situation.

DREAMS AND INTUITION

The guidance, intuitive insights, and mysterious journeys we embark on to far-away realms may indeed be the most exciting part of dreaming. Our dream adventures and encounters can be miraculous and offer us immense guidance and support. Some dreams give you deeper insights into certain situations in your life, and others may even come with strong premonitions about events that are about to happen. You can fine-tune your intuition and ability to better understand the messages in your dreams by staying aware and present in your daily life and paying close attention to situations that may remind you of something from a dream. In this way, you become even more receptive to messages coming your way. Dreams do not stop when we wake up; rather, the energy of dreams continues throughout the day. By becoming more observant of the world around us, we may find symbols that remind us of images from our inner dream world appearing in the most unexpected places. When our inner and outer worlds collaborate to create messages for us, we experience meaningful coincidences known as *synchronicity*. We will return to this luminous form of guidance later in the book.

Introduction

DREAMS AND AFFIRMATIONS

When you listen to your dreams, emotional reactions and situations of which you may not yet be aware rise to the surface. This process helps clear out the dissonance that so often occurs when you are having an unconscious reaction to situations in life. You may have a deep underlying feeling that clashes with an unconscious reaction and end up feeling overwhelmed without even knowing why or how. If you don't process your reactions, emotional blockages are created, and they trap and weigh you down and make it much more difficult to manifest and affirm positive developments in your life. Even if you were to think positive thoughts in those situations, there is not enough space to stay positive because the negative weight is pulling you down.

Dream work helps you develop a much better understanding of your true underlying feelings. By helping you see what is going on in your life, emotional blockages are released. With all this new space, you now have the room you need to attract more positive thoughts into your daily life and remain positive. When you can stay on a higher frequency, you now begin to build a unique tool kit—the power to create the life you desire!

When we know what we want, and the energy is flowing, we begin to resonate on that level, and we are now choosing the thoughts that are serving us in the best possible way. Dreams help us embark on our true paths and fill us with the energy we need to continue in the right direction. We become more receptive to our higher self's guidance and develop the inner power to create our dream life.

1

Jungian Dream Psychology

The world of dream psychology is a fascinating place. Many different branches of psychology today embrace and invite dreams into the therapy room. Even though there are many wondrous dream theories, any dream book would be incomplete without honoring the clinical contributions made by Sigmund Freud and Carl Jung.

SIGMUND FREUD AND CARL JUNG

Both Sigmund Freud and Carl Jung played significant roles in the development of depth psychology, and even though they differed in their approach, they both emphasized the value of dreams. Sigmund Freud is often referred to as the father of psychoanalysis. He did indeed contribute significantly to dream psychology by introducing us to the concept of the unconscious and the importance of dreaming. Carl Jung and Freud worked together for some time, but Jung soon developed an even broader understanding of dreams with a higher emphasis on the spiritual dimensions. Freud may have called dreams "the royal road to the unconscious," but, in contrast to Jung, Freud used dreams primarily to help his patients become aware of their repressed sexual desires, which, according to Freud, were at the root of all neurotic disturbances.[1] Whereas Freud viewed dreams as wish fulfillments and very much related them to suppressed sexuality, Jung viewed dreams as a product of our total psyche, i.e., as not only as coming from our unconscious, but rather as also having major influences from the collective unconscious, the field shared by all of us, and also as helping us form more complete perspectives and become better as individuals.[2]

Jung's profound dream teachings inspire many of the concepts discussed in this book. In this chapter, we will look at some of Jung's remarkable contributions to the world of depth psychology and see how Jung built a beautiful foundation to understand our dreams. We will begin with the powerful concept of the collective unconscious, which, spiritually, can be compared to some of the dimensions found in the astral plane. It is indeed the backbone of much of Jungian dream psychology and helps us understand how we can tap into so much information while sleeping.

THE COLLECTIVE UNCONSCIOUS

Thought of by many people today as the astral plane, Jung referred to this majestic field that connects us all and is present within all living beings, as the collective unconscious.[3] This is the field we tap into when we dream. It is of particular interest in Jungian depth psychology, as it shows how dreams, coincidences, and symbolic connections do not always originate within our unconscious, but also in this connected energy field, hence explaining how we can sometimes dream of events to which we have no connection in any way in our daily lives.

Jung was one of the pioneers of this concept and often talked about how many of his inspirations came from this unconscious realm. He said it is because we visit this field when we dream that our dreams sometimes bring about ideas or symbols that are foreign to our personal lives but may have been of significance to humanity at some other point in time.[4] This concept brings some clarity into how we sometimes dream of something very abstract and symbolic, such as a dragon or a sacred scripture, without ever having consciously experienced anything of that nature in our own lives. Or we may dream about some event that was influenced by a myth from another part of the world, but that was somehow "translated" into a situation that made more sense to us. We may also have a premonition about an event that hasn't even happened yet or would have been impossible for us to foresee in waking life. These experiences show the significance of this interrelated field and how connected we all are. We will revisit these types of phenomena later in the book in the chapters about synchronicity and intuition.

OUR PSYCHE

In the Jungian school of thought, our psyche has four dimensions.[5] In the middle of our psyche is the archetype of Self. The Self is the regulating center of the *entire psyche* and helps us feel whole.[6] It is commonly referred to today as our higher self. On the other hand, our ego is only at the center of our *personal consciousness*, i.e., not the entire psyche. It is important to make a strong note here that our ego is only conscious of what is within our personal consciousness, which further highlights the value of dreams, as they help enhance the flow between our unconscious and conscious parts and help bring higher awareness of both our inner and outer worlds.

Personal Dimension
Personal consciousness includes the content of which we are aware. The ego is at the center of the personal consciousness. *The personal unconscious* comprises content that is personal to us but is not yet conscious, or is forgotten or repressed.

Collective Dimension
The collective consciousness relates to the cultural values that have been built up and shared over time and are now shared by all humans.

The collective unconscious is a field shared by all living beings that exists beyond both time and space. In Jungian psychology, the collective unconscious comprises the archetypes, the universal patterns of behavior that influence us with their energy patterns.[7] Depending on our upbringing and culture, archetypal images and themes are revealed to us in our dreams in a way that makes sense to us. That's why many fairy tales around the world are based on similar principles but feature different story characters. It is also why many of our dreams are similar, such as being chased by a monster or nurtured by a mother. An archetype that often shows up in dreams is the Wise Old Man. The specific archetypal image of the Wise Old Man will vary, depending on the culture in which he shows up. A Hindu may see him as a guru, whereas a Christian may see him as a certain saint, and a Buddhist as a monk or as Buddha himself. Whether we call it the astral plane or the collective unconscious, it is a fascinating field filled with universal wisdom. Best of all—we tap into it every night when we sleep.

INDIVIDUATION

Perhaps of most significance in all of Jung's psychological concepts when it comes to dream work is the process of *individuation*. Individuation allows us to grow and become all that we can be. Because the unconscious is so enormous, it may not be possible to achieve full individuation, at least not while we are alive, as we will always have some aspect of ego present within us. The ego is only conscious of our personal consciousness. Jung said that the importance does not lie in the amount of the achievement but rather in being on the path itself.[8] Listening to our dreams is a vital function of the path of individuation, as individuation involves a beautiful dialogue between our ego and our higher self. The term "the transcendent function" refers to an enhanced flow between our unconscious and conscious side, and this communication is enhanced when we work with our dreams.[9]

It is our higher self that directs our dreams and sends messages and insights to our conscious part. The symbols in our dreams are carefully selected from all dimensions of our psyche, including the collective unconscious, to best get the message across. The more we work on our emotional imbalances, the more receptive we become to the higher guidance available to us. We can then spend more of our dream time tapping into miraculous wisdom and blossom into the best expression of ourselves.

JUNG'S INSPIRATIONS

Much of dream psychology as we know it today was inspired by Jung and his remarkable theories. Jung introduced the world to some magnificent and highly insightful concepts, inspired by many different areas, including Romantic philosophy, depth psychology, religion, alchemy, and mysticism.

Jung was also strongly influenced by his mother's interest and experiences in the paranormal. He also experienced many paranormal events of his own, which he writes about in his autobiography *Memories, Dreams, Reflections.*[10] It was Jung's mother who introduced him to Eastern religions, and he studied Hindu yogic traditions, Zen Buddhism, Taoism, and Tibetan teachings.

In his memoir, Jung shared how he particularly appreciated the Eastern way of emphasizing the inner life rather than the outer. Jung's profound approach to our psyche is a major influencer behind many psychological theories and forms the basis of many of the concepts shared in this book.

2

Dream Characters

Although you may occasionally have dreams about humanity as a whole, most of your dreams are unique to yourself and are primarily concerned with *you*. Because your personal experiences play such a crucial role in each dream, it will always be difficult for even the most seasoned dream analyst to fully understand your dreams. We all share some universal dream themes from time to time, and we will look at some popular dream interpretation examples together later in this book. The examples provided in the dream interpretation guide in chapter 8 have been chosen carefully, with a specific set of questions suggested around each dream theme to help you develop your dream interpretation process.

To help you build a better understanding of how to best work with your dreams, this chapter introduces you to some of the most central aspects of dreaming: dreams of ourselves, dreams of people we know, and dreams of unknown people.

DREAMS OF OURSELVES AND OTHERS— OUR PERSONA AND SHADOW

Dreams are multidimensional and can bring many messages for us, from both subjective and objective angles. As we will see in the next chapter, some of our dreams also vibrate with higher soul wisdom. On the subjective level, dreams revolve around your inner drama, and the dream figures in subjective dreams have been chosen to represent unknown aspects of yourself. On the objective level, dream figures may instead have been chosen to help highlight an interaction that is currently going on between you and other people in your life or to help you gain insight into your relationships with others. Almost all our dreams feature some type of character. As a general rule of thumb, the majority of our dreams are subjective, and the figures in such dreams represent a part of ourselves (even when we dream of people we know). Each person in a subjective dream has been chosen very carefully to highlight something present within us. We will look at subjective and objective dream angles in more detail in the next chapter.

The Persona

We all have different aspects of our personality within us. By developing a better understanding of ourselves and the roles we play in the outer world, it becomes much easier to see what the dream is trying to tell us. Two well-known Jungian concepts are our *persona* and our *shadow*. These aspects are important as they illustrate how we present ourselves to the world (our persona or mask) and what we are hiding (our shadow).[1] Do you know which side of yourself you present to others in different situations? When we are connected to our higher self, and there is a healthy flow within our psyche, our persona will be well-balanced. Certain situations require us to adapt to society slightly differently, depending on what we are doing. For example, many social roles carry certain expectations, both from ourselves and those around us, such as mother, father, wife, husband, doctor, police officer, etc. As we develop our ego, we choose various persona roles and integrate them into our ego-identity.

If we put too much of our energy into our persona or our outer roles in life, we may feel empty, as though there were no real person inside us. In those situations, our ego is no longer governed by our higher self, but we now place too much emphasis on our outer roles. We are imbalanced! For example, a businessman who stays working late in the office every night feels empty when he is not working. He has over-identified with his corporate role and lacks a true sense of identity. On the other hand, if we do not sufficiently develop our persona, we easily become hurt by even the smallest situations. We need to have a balanced inner and outer expression.

The Shadow

Awareness is indeed the key in any self-growth process, and our dreams are here to help us. Perhaps of even more importance, when it comes to identifying different aspects of ourselves, the shadow is the part that we are not aware of. Besides having a persona, we also have a shadow,[2] which is the part of ourselves that we are hiding from ourselves and others (although others are more likely to see it than we are!). The shadow contains aspects of ourselves that we have unconsciously repressed, either because we did not like those traits or thought others did not like them. Our shadow is often personified in dream characters and is projected onto people in our daily lives and surrounding environment. By working with the projections we make onto other people or objects in our dreams, we can better understand our own shadow.

For example, we may project our shadow onto someone we dislike or envy onto a dream character. By analyzing the characters in our dreams, we often see that they have qualities that are also present within ourselves.

DREAMS OF UNKNOWN PEOPLE

Sometimes the people in our dreams are total strangers, and an unknown man or woman may even be taking center stage. Again, it is important to remind ourselves that most characters that enter our dream world have been carefully chosen to highlight something going on with us.

The unknown man or woman may represent the feminine and masculine aspects within ourselves. The Jungian terms for these archetypal forces are *anima* and *animus*. You may have come across these terms in everyday discussions with associates at work, with friends, or even in popular magazines.

The anima is the feminine archetype within a man, and the animus is the masculine archetype within a woman.[3] We tend to project our anima/animus on people of the opposite sex. When we are experiencing this type of projection, we may feel that we have fallen in love, and we often feel rather fascinated by those on whom we project our anima/animus image.

Although anima/animus projection often begins with mesmerizing and idealization, it can easily turn into disgust and annoyance, as we see parts of ourselves that we don't like. That is when our shadow emerges. Being aware of this type of projection as it shows up in our dreams can later protect us from pain and tears. True love is not a projection but a constant state of being.

By working with all aspects of ourselves and continuously turning to our dreams, we develop a much higher awareness of ourselves, which reduces the risks of becoming lost in this projection process. The feminine and masculine sides of ourselves are often in conflict, and they are always trying to achieve perfect harmony. Dreams of an unknown man or an unknown woman may help you see how well you are balancing your energies and whether or not you are utilizing them both to your highest potential.

If you are a woman and dream of an unknown man, it may be your animus or masculine part of yourself that is showing up. Your masculine side represents the autonomous part of yourself and the ability to be assertive and go after what you want. If the unknown man is nice to you, or if you are making love, this could signify that you are doing a good job integrating your male energies into your life right now. If an unknown man is chasing you, you may be running away from your masculine qualities, and you may need to stand your ground a bit more and become more autonomous.

If you are a man and dream of an unknown woman, this may be your anima or feminine side of yourself. Your feminine side represents your ability to be more receiving, caring, intuitive, and even philosophical. If the woman in the dream is weak or vulnerable, it may mean that you need to strengthen your feminine side. It could also be a message for you to listen more to your intuition. Jung's notion of anima and animus helps bring more clarity about why we so often encounter an unknown man or woman in our dreams. Of course, the dream could also flow with guidance on a higher soul level, and in those instances, the unknown man or woman could be bringing sacred wisdom into your life.

Dreams truly have the potential to help bring awareness of all aspects of ourselves. We not only develop higher self-knowledge and a healthier connection with our higher self, but we also release emotional blockages in the process. Best of all, when we listen to our dreams, we become more open to our miraculous guidance and blossom into our authentic selves.

3

Dream Connection: A Step-by-Step Guide

Dreams can be very puzzling and confusing. It is no wonder we sometimes feel overwhelmed from not being able to "make sense" of our dreams. We may even brush them away as nonsense. Whatever kinds of dreams you are having, they all provide you with powerful guidance one way or the other. All dreams are valuable, not only the "big" ones. Even the "little" dreams help in some form. Even if you are not receiving inspirational guidance in the form of the most soul-touching messages in a dream, it doesn't mean you are not growing. Instead, the dream may help you heal emotionally and allow you to process unconscious emotional feelings and reactions.

Embracing a loving connection with your dreams beautifully illuminates your path of inner soul growth and is also a wondrous way to restore your emotional well-being. Developing an appreciation of dreams not only magnifies and heightens your awareness but also has the potential of helping you see life situations with more clarity. Dreams help you see the truth. Dreams help pinpoint what is going on in your life and connect with your feelings, which ultimately helps you develop acceptance, understanding, and compassion for yourself. Ultimately, dreams open up new windows for your inner soul dream to unfold.

Dreams help us become aware of emotional patterns that we may be stuck in by weaving together life experiences that vibrate with the same emotional energy. Some life events carry intense emotional feelings, which may sometimes be difficult to embrace in waking life. With the guiding hand of a luminous dream, we are led to a safe place to explore the feelings in the dream. When viewed from a higher lens of dreaming, feelings that otherwise would have been too difficult to accept can be safely explored and processed, and this is how true healing begins.

BENEFITS OF EMBRACING YOUR DREAMS:

1. Dreams play an honest picture of what is truly going on in your life, without filters and emotional protection barriers
2. Dreams encourage you to explore intense issues from a safe and protected place
3. Dreams help you see how you truly feel, even if it's uncomfortable to acknowledge in waking life
4. Dreams bring about higher self-awareness and self-knowledge

5. Dreams bring about a deeper understanding of emotional patterns and habits
6. Dreams help cleanse out emotional debris and clear the space for personal growth
7. Dreams can help show how you are growing
8. Dreams can be life-changing and bring about transformational shifts
9. Dreams offer guidance and insight
10. Dreams bring about a loving connection with your higher self
11. Dreams help you connect with your soul's home
12. Dreams boost your creativity
13. Dreams encourage problem-solving
14. Working with your dreams is fun!

SYMBOLIC LANGUAGE

Your journeys to dream realms are filled with adventures designed to help you along the way. By taking the time to work with your dreams and interpret the symbols, you can find helpful messages in the most unexpected places.

There are a couple of points to remember before we begin connecting with our dreams:

1. Dreams are not made up of the same language we use in our daily lives. The dream world relies on a more *symbolic language*, which is made up of images that our unconscious selves have carefully selected to communicate something important to us. Because dreams are symbolic by nature, they are not linear in any way. That is why we often feel confused by all the different scenes.

2. Dreams are *multidimensional*, and there is no "one-size-fits-all" type of interpretation approach. If, for example, you know someone whose thumb has been amputated and then dream about a missing thumb, the associations you make with the dream will be very different from someone who doesn't have a personal connection with such an image. Likewise, you may dream about an ocean, but how you *feel* in the dream often helps bring out the dream's underlying message. If you felt frightened by your dream ocean, it would have a whole different meaning than if you were inspired by it. Dream dictionaries can be useful first resources, but they will often provide you with only one possible association. In reality, you may have a very different personal association that is much more fitted to your life situation. That being said, certain common dream themes are often shared among all of us, such as falling, going back to school, being chased, etc. We will look at some of these dreams later in the book and see how you can use these examples in your dream connection process.

The context in which the dream occurs can also give you many clues. Ask yourself, "What is the relevance of the dream in my life right now?" "How did the dream make me feel?" "Where in my life do I feel like that?"

DREAM CONNECTION STEPS

The dream connection steps below have been developed from years of extensive dream studies and from working with many people's dreams, both from a spiritual and an emotional growth perspective. Last but not least, from my nightly dream voyages. The steps below offer a way to compassionately connect with your dreams while also integrating the Jungian process of making associations and amplifying symbols to see how the associations best fit into your life right now.[1]

>Step 1: Write down the dream
>Step 2: What type of dream is it?
>Step 3: Make associations
>Step 4: Explore the dream
>Step 5: How does your dream relate to your waking life?
>Step 6: Honor your dream

STEP 1: WRITE THE DREAM IN YOUR DREAM JOURNAL

The insights that come from writing down your dreams cannot be emphasized enough. Writing is a transformative process that helps connect our inner and outer worlds in a very symbolic way. Write the dream in the present tense, as if it is happening right now. What is happening? Where is the dream taking place? What is the scene like? Is it light or dark? Who is in the dream? What is the outcome? How are you feeling in the dream? Telling the dream in present tense helps keep the dream alive and makes it easier to experience all dream elements. As you remember your dream, look around carefully and include any details you see and experience. Always reflect upon how you feel in the dream. Emotions are powerful in dreams and can be used as stepping stones for deeper connection and understanding.

Step 2: Categorize Your Dream—What Type of Dream Is It?

When working with our dreams, it is helpful to look at them from different perspectives. First, we have the kinds of dreams that help us grow on a personal level. These dreams originate in our minds and tend to fall under the psychological or emotional processing lens. I refer to these dreams as being subjective or objective. Then we have the types of dreams that help us grow on a timeless soul level. I think of these dreams as our soul dreams. Here we have our intuitive guidance dreams and our astral travel dreams.

Popular subsets of dream categories include wish-fulfillment dreams, lucid dreams, recurrent dreams, and nightmares. Thinking about what type of dream you are working with can be helpful as you begin to explore your dream. As dreams as multi-dimensional, it is also possible that some dreams have a bit of all elements woven together in different layers.

PERSONAL GROWTH DREAMS

Dream Type 1 – The Subjective Dream: *Know Thyself!*

Most of our dreams are subjective in one way or the other in that they are designed to help enhance our self-knowledge while also helping us process our emotions and feelings. In a subjective dream, the dream characters represent different parts of you and have been carefully chosen to highlight qualities present within you. In other words, you are projecting aspects of yourself onto characters in the dream so that you can more easily see that these qualities are also within you! If an angry man is chasing you in your dreams, think about what you may be running away from. Perhaps you feel frightened by your aggressive behaviors. You may not even be aware of what you are hiding. These types of dreams are helpful tools for finding out and learning more about yourself. As a general rule of thumb, when there is something slightly different about the people in your dream from their "ordinary" appearance in daily life, they have probably been chosen to represent certain qualities within you, so think about what stands out about the characters. What comes to mind when you think of this person? How do their actions in the dream remind you about yourself?

Dream Type 2 – The Objective Dream: *Relationship with Others and Emotional Processing*

Sometimes dreams are more objective in nature and can indeed be about the other person or the relationship you have with that person. In an objective dream, the dream characters have entered your dream as themselves and have been chosen to highlight the interaction, communication, and issues between you. The characters could also have been chosen to help you process different emotional reactions and underlying feelings. If, for example, you are arguing with your partner, the dream could be helping you to understand better how you feel about a certain situation and help you see the situation from different perspectives. By letting the feelings come to the surface, you also release energetic blockages.

SOUL DREAMS

Dream Type 3 – The Intuitive Dream
Intuitive Guidance to Help You Prepare for Life Events or Guide You in a Certain Direction

Intuitive dreams help guide you through times of growth and may give you profound messages. Some dreams may even be telepathic if other people or dreamers convey the messages. Most guidance in intuitive dreams, however, is delivered through your inner divine connection. As a general rule, if the dream has a good "sequence," i.e., the scenes more or less follow a story line and don't feel as confusing as other dreams, or if you feel as though you're "observing" the dream, rather than participating in it, and you have no major emotional reactions, it could be an intuitive guidance dream. It should be noted, though, that sometimes guidance dreams don't follow storylines at all. The best way to listen to your guidance is to familiarize yourself with all types of dreams you have and keep a journal of all your dream patterns, themes, and stories. In this category of dreams, we also have synchronistic dreams. These dreams miraculously bring together images, symbols, or events from your inner world (such as a dream image) with a corresponding event or symbol in your outer world. Such powerful coincidences help guide you in the right direction, and they also show how there is no real separation between our inner and outer worlds.

Dream Type 4 – The Astral Dream
Help from Your Guides and Visits to Other Realms

Along with synchronistic and intuitive dreams, astral dreams also help us understand that we may not always be "inside our minds" at night, but we may sometimes go on sacred journeys into other dream realms. Again, we can see how the separation between the different night realms may not be as clear as we first think. In these types of dream journeys, you may visit faraway places, fairylands, historical venues, or you may also meet with a sacred teacher. You may meet with deceased relatives and friends, angels, and spirit guides. Dragons, mermaids, and fairies often show up in astral dreams as well. Astral dreams offer powerful guidance and unique wisdom. As we saw in the earlier chapters about Jungian psychology, the notion of a collective unconscious fits hand in hand with the dimensions we visit in astral dreams. Often, astral journeys are lucid, which means that you are fully aware of dreaming while dreaming.

DREAM SUB-CATEGORIES

The Wish-Fulfillment Dream
What would we do without wish-fulfillment dreams! These miraculous night voyages help us experience what it feels like to have our dreams come true. Best of all,

we now have the power to tap into the vibrational frequency required to attract the same energy into our lives. The power of a clear mind, without doubt, and worry, is immensely powerful. When you learn how to capture the confidence that comes from wish-fulfillment dreams, the world is your oyster. We will revisit this concept in chapter ten.

The Lucid Dream

To be lucid when dreaming means that you are aware that you are dreaming while dreaming. Lucid dreams sometimes happen spontaneously, and we often wake up as soon as we realize we are dreaming. However, with practice, you can learn to remain asleep and even invite more lucid dreams. By testing yourself a few times throughout the day to see if you are dreaming, you can bring this consciousness into the dream world. You can, for example, try to take an extra high jump up in the air and see what happens, or you can move your hand around quickly and check how many fingers you have. If you are interested in exploring lucid dreaming, I recommend checking out Clare Johnson, Robert Waggoner, and Gregory Scott Sparrow's works.

The Recurrent Dream

Some dreams come back around. Recurrent dreams sometimes come about to help you see something that is going on, but you have been unable to understand for some reason. It is not uncommon for recurrent dreams to relate to events that happened a long time ago. The dream is coming back in this instance because you are still reliving the same emotional pattern, and the dream is here to help you see it. Recurring dreams are very important, as they highlight something that is going on and is possibly even being recreated over and over because we have not yet worked it out.

Recurrent dreams are most often subjective, i.e., they concern something going on within you, but sometimes they can also be objective in that they highlight patterns you're recreating with others. They can occasionally also be both intuitive and astral, if you're not listening to the messages revealed to you. Although, these types of recurrent dreams are less common.

The Nightmare

A nightmare is a desperate cry for attention from your higher self. You are not getting the message, so the dream has now turned into something incredibly strong and terrifying to ensure that you are listening. The nightmare is not your enemy but rather your friend. Nightmares come about to help us heal by highlighting urgent situations that we need to attend to.

Nightmares evoke intense emotional reactions within us and are so frightening that they wake us up with a startle. They can be both subjective and objective and often revolve around unprocessed feelings and emotions. They may also highlight particular situations that are damaging in our lives. As we will discuss further in chapter 5, they can also be astral.

Dream Connection: A Step-by-Step Guide

STEP 3: MAKE ASSOCIATIONS WITH DREAM SYMBOLS AND CHARACTERS

Now that you have identified what type of dream you are likely working with, you can continue exploring the symbols in your dream and see what associations come to mind. Your unconscious has chosen each symbol in the dream for a reason, so it helps reflect upon what you associate each symbol, event, or feeling with. For example, if you dreamt of a dolphin in the water, write down details about what a dolphin means to you and what you associate water with. Remember to go back to each dream image in this exercise, i.e., make associations from each image or event; do not continue with a "free association." A free association would be when you first make an association with water and then continue to associate that association with something else. It is better to work with the original image, as, after all, that is how your dream has chosen to communicate something to your conscious self.

Making associations to dream elements and symbols can be very helpful in the dream connection process. Associations can help link the dream element to experiences that the dream may have drawn upon and help you see how the dream may relate to your waking life.

STEP 4: HOW DOES YOUR DREAM RELATE TO YOUR LIFE RIGHT NOW?

Think about what is happening in your life. Reflecting upon how the dream may relate to your emotions and experiences in waking life is another valuable step of the dream connection process. Why did it come about now?

Think of the dream from both a subjective and objective perspective. If the dream relates to your inner emotional life, how does it show what may be happening in your inner landscape? A dream can also be explored from a more objective perspective, where characters in the dream represent themselves. You can then reflect on your interaction with others or examine habits and patterns.

Subjective Dream

If it is a subjective dream, how is the dream highlighting some unknown or repressed aspect about yourself? Think about how you were feeling in the dream. Have you had a similar feeling in your waking life?

Objective Dream

If it is an objective dream, is the dream helping you better deal with a situation by processing your feelings? Or is it maybe giving you another perspective? What is going on in your life right now, and why did this dream come just now?

Intuitive Dream

If it is an intuitive dream, you may be called to pay careful attention to some events. How could these insights be of help to you right now? Pay close attention to any messages that feel valuable on your path of soul growth.

Astral Dream

If it is an astral dream and you're being visited by deceased relatives, spirit guides, or beings from other realms, what is the message for you? Why did you have this experience now? You may also have tapped into sacred universal wisdom in a very special dream journey or initiation. Treasure your astral dreams; they are inner golden treasure chests.

Wish-Fulfillment Dream

Wish fulfillment dreams tend to occur at moments in time when you need a little extra push and maybe an encouraging pat on the shoulder. How can you relive the powerful feeling of having your wish come true in the dream? Wish dreams can also help you heal from not being able to get what you wish for in your daily life and instead let you experience having it come true in your dreams. The actual scenario in the dream is not as important as the feeling of having your wishes fulfilled.

Lucid Dream

Lucid dreams are exceptionally powerful in that you can use your conscious mind when interpreting them, and you often have some type of ability to alter dream scenes, which helps you practice the power of positive thinking.

Recurrent Dream

What is the message you are not getting? Or do you already know what the issue is but hope it will go away? Until you have sorted out the situation, your dreams will come back in recurrent form, and they may even develop into different story lines with the same theme as they try to highlight the issue from new angles.

Nightmare

If you don't listen to the messages in your "regular" dreams or work out the issues in recurrent dreams, your dreams can quickly escalate into nightmares. Nightmares are a serious cry for help, so you must pay close attention to these dreams and see why they have come about. We'll return to nightmares in chapter 5.

STEP 5: EXPLORE THE DREAM

You can explore and connect with your dream deeply by entering the dream and dreaming the dream forward. It can be a very empowering process that spread positive reverberations in all aspects of your life. Exploring dreams can also involve re-entering the dream and engaging directly with dream elements and characters, either interacting and talking with a character or symbol or role-playing by experiencing the dream from the perspective of the dream character or dream element.

You can also draw images from the dream. The process of connecting our unconscious and conscious in the form of drawing is very powerful. Bringing a dream memory into form opens up the opportunity to directly experience the dream. Dreams are symbolic and visual, and drawing the dream helps to keep the creative aspect of the dream alive.

STEP 6: HONOR YOUR DREAM

Asking yourself if you would like to honor the dream in some way can be an enchanting part of the dream connection process. Perhaps there is a transformational life change unfolding in your life. Consciously reflecting upon how your dreams are helping you during your soul growth can be immensely enriching.

Whatever type of dream you are having, remember you are having this dream at this particular moment in time for a reason. The more you work with your dreams, the more you will start seeing themes and messages shining through your daily life. Write down as many dreams you can remember each morning, and keep at it. By looking at dreams as a series, you can see how they change over time. Keep your dreams alive, and look back in your dream journal from time to time. When you come across something in your daily life that reminds you of a dream image, add those experiences as notes in your journal as well. As you enhance your awareness, you become more receptive to guidance both in your dreams and the outer world. By adding corresponding events from your daily life, as well as any other insights that may come to mind, to your dream journal, your dreams will be enriched, or, as Jung would say, "amplified," and you never know where this beautiful process will take you![2]

*Every **great day** begins with a **great intention**.*

4

Dreamy Intentions

The amazing journeys we embark on in our dreams and the powerful guidance given to us in these realms and planes can be mesmerizing, but what if you don't remember your dreams? If your dreams fly by you as soon as you wake up, don't despair! It happens to even the most seasoned dream workers. This chapter will look at some things you can do to better keep your dreams fresh in your mind as you wake up. The best remedy for deeper sleep and more dreams is to reduce the intake of mind-altering substances, including caffeine and alcohol, so try to experiment living without caffeine and alcohol for a few weeks and see what happens to your dreams.

Reasons for poor dream recall:
1. Insufficient sleep—many people do not sleep eight hours per night. This stems from being exposed to artificial blue light from electronic

devices before sleep, which suppresses melatonin production.
2. Waking up too early (and going to bed too late!)—our REM periods of sleep build up in longer increments through the night. The richest period of our dream cycles is in the early morning hours.
3. Being under the influence of alcohol and drugs leads to poorer quality of sleep with reduced REM sleep.
4. Taking sleeping pills—over-the-counter sleep aid could decrease deep sleep and suppress REM sleep.[1]
5. Not valuing our dreams—when we begin paying attention to our dreams, they respond!

Whether or not you remember your dreams, you can rest assured that you dream—a lot! On average, we have about three to five dreams per night. So, even if you don't recall your dreams, are they still helpful? Yes! Dreams help you process unconscious reactions and emotions, so your unconscious side always benefits from your dreams. However, suppose you don't recall them in the morning. In that case, you miss out on the healthy awareness enhancing flow that would otherwise occur between your unconscious and conscious sides—not to mention all the beautiful messages, inspiration, and guidance that will pass you by. Without dream images clear in your mind and heart, it will be more difficult to identify guidance in your outer world as it happens, as you will not be able to experience the remarkable coincidences or synchronistic events that occur when something in your daily life miraculously coincides with something you have just dreamt about.

When you can reflect upon and truly work with your dreams, the processing becomes conscious and stays with you. With enhanced awareness levels, you will not only feel better (because you have fewer unconscious emotional reactions), but you will also become more receptive to the guidance all around you.

DEEPER SLEEP AND BETTER DREAM RECALL

If you are not sleeping well, here are some methods that have proven helpful for many people I've worked with over the years. Explore and see if any of these resonate with you, and of course, keep adding to the list if you find something that works even better.

Ways to promote deep sleep and enhance your dream recall:

- Turn your bedroom into a blissful spa. Mist your room in soothing lavender. Create a peaceful ritual every night before going to sleep, such as taking a relaxing sea salt bath and enjoy a cup of chamomile or lavender tea.
- Remove any clutter from your bedroom. Keep your bedroom clean, peaceful, and fresh. This is your sacred space for sleeping.

- Place some calming and loving crystals on your nightstand: Amethyst, celestite, Herkimer diamond, lapis lazuli, rose quartz, and clear quartz.
- Keep any electronic devices out of your bedroom, including televisions. Melatonin is naturally released in your body when it gets dark. Bright light, including blue light from electronic devices, suppresses the production of melatonin.
- Listen to serene relaxation music that helps you calm down and rewind.
- Honor your sleep by keeping a regular sleep schedule, going to bed at the same time every night, and waking up at the same time every morning. Living in alignment with nature does wonders for our sleep.
- Flow and grow—honor your body with a light yoga practice in the morning, and go for a 20-minute brisk walk each day. Make time also to enjoy two or three longer nature walks each week.
- Begin each day with a meditation practice—give yourself a few moments of bliss in the morning, with silent meditation, and meet each day from a place of inner soul connection. This will help you stay emotionally calm throughout the day.
- Practice mindfulness and a few soothing yoga asanas throughout the day to keep your body flexible and your mind open. Legs up the wall pose, with your back body resting on the ground, is great for preparing your body for sleep.

Dreamy Intentions

- Before going to bed, spend some moments again in a clear meditation. When you take the time to clear your mind before going to bed, there is less need to work through emotional clutter while you're sleeping. We bring the consciousness we go to bed with into our sleep. A nightly meditation practice opens up the room for deep sleep and good dreams.
- When you go to bed, set an intention of going to bed with clear consciousness and remembering your dreams.
- Avoid alcohol and drugs
- Avoid fatty and salty foods late at night, as well as anything spicy.
- Foods great for sleep include coconut and almond milk, nuts, beans, chickpeas, bananas, potatoes, and cherries; foods rich in magnesium: pumpkin seeds, almonds, cashews, spinach; foods rich in calcium: sesame seeds, hard cheese, almonds, sardines, edamame; vegetables high in dietary fiber—prebiotics: leeks, onions, lentils, cabbage, and artichokes.*
- Keep a dream journal by your bed and a pen nearby. When you wake up, take some time to lie still in bed while thinking about your dreams. I recommend keeping the journal nearby so that you can easily reach for it. Dreams often disappear once we start moving around and quickly fade

---

* Please seek advice from a licensed dietician to make sure you are getting a balanced diet that is beneficial for your body.

as the minutes go by, so it is important to write down whatever you can recall as soon as possible. Write down anything you can remember, even if it is just a glimpse of a scene.

- Keep your dream alive by reflecting upon it as you go about your day. If something happens in your daily life that reminds you of your dream, add a note in your dream journal.
- Go to bed with the intention to remember your dreams when you wake up in the morning! By having this intention as your drift off to sleep, you will program yourself to remember your dreams.
- You can also ask your dreams for guidance around a particular question or subject. The more attention you give your dreams, the better they will respond. You may also wish to write down this question in your journal. Remember that dreams can seem very confusing at first. There is no need to filter and try to "make sense" of them as you recall them. Just write down whatever you can remember. Once you have recorded your dream, you can start connecting with it (see chapter 3 for some useful tips):
- What types of emotions did you experience in the dream?
- What type of dream is it?
- What associations can you make with the symbols/events/people in the dream?
- How does the dream relate to your life right now?
- Do you want to explore the dream further?

Dreamy Intentions

- How can you honor your dream?

By practicing and being persistent, you can program and train yourself to better remember your dreams at night. Writing down your dreams in the morning, and asking your dreams for guidance at night, is a wonderful way of enhancing the flow.

DREAM INCUBATION

You can ask your dreams for guidance about anything that's on your mind. Perhaps you need direction or help with your career, love life, finances, or health. Or maybe you want to develop your intuitive abilities and be more open to premonitions and synchronicities coming your way. *Dream Incubation* is the term used to describe the process of asking your dreams for guidance. When you go to bed, develop a clear intention, and write down the question in your dream journal. There is a special power that develops from actually writing down a question. It is recommended that you only ask one question per night, as the messages can be very difficult to identify otherwise. Dreams are often confusing, to begin with, so there is no need to complicate the process!

When you wake up in the morning, write down anything you can remember from the night, even if you don't think your dreams have answered your question. Once you take the time to process the dreams, you will start to see answers shining through! Keep the dream alive through the day, and be alert to any events in the outer world that remind you of a dream image. When you ask your dreams for guidance, stay open to even wider answers. The wisdom you are tapping into from the astral plane is infinite. You may get answers that go way beyond what you originally asked if that is what your higher self knows will be in your best interest.

There is an ancient saying that so beautifully tells us . . .

"When the pupil is ready, the teacher will appear."

Your dreams provide you with the knowledge you need when you are ready to receive it!

CRYSTAL CLEAR DREAMS

Crystals have been used worldwide for thousands of years for their manifestation and healing abilities, and they are also beautiful dream enhancers. Life energy flows within and around you, and the unique energy vibrations from crystals have stimulating influences on your energy field. You can use crystals of a certain color and a certain frequency to aid dream recall and enhance your visits to dream realms.

Amethyst

Amethyst helps clear the aura and is a wonderful peaceful crystal that spreads harmony all around. If you feel anxious or worried that someone may be sending negative energy your way, it is a beautiful crystal to place under the pillow or on the nightstand. The amethyst lovingly transforms negativity into positive energy and helps calm you down by releasing tension. It is also a good helper if you have insomnia. Also, it helps open the crown chakra, your higher awareness energy center above your head, and makes you more receptive to the guidance coming your way.

Aventurine

The Aventurine crystal is a wonderful heart opener and helps you find trust and the inner knowing that all is working out. Suppose you are experiencing feelings of anger during the day. In that case, it is a wonderful crystal to place on your heart chakra, the loving energy center around your heart area, as it helps clear and balances energies. Aventurine is also a powerful dream enhancer that stimulates dreaming and helps you release impatience. With trust in the outcome, you now have the power to make your dreams come true!

Moldavite

The Moldavite crystal was formed from rocks melting and merging with a giant meteorite that touched down in Eastern Europe over 15 million years ago. It is a high-vibration multidimensional crystal that helps develop your intuition, as well as wish-fulfillment abilities, by connecting you to higher planes and astral energies. It is particularly powerful when placed on the third eye chakra, the intuitive energy center between your eyebrows.

Tourmaline

This powerful crystal is a beautiful wisdom and love stone filled with inspiration, which also helps clear and purify energies all around. It comes in many colors. The blue tourmaline helps to activate your third-eye chakra—your clairvoyance and intuition center. So if you would like to dream more intuitive dreams, this is a great stone to place under your pillow. The green tourmaline inspires creativity and helps you dream of possible solutions to a problem. The pink tourmaline is a precious love stone that inspires you to trust in love. It helps you let go of negative feeling patterns in the heart and transforms these patterns into new, loving energies. The green and pink tourmalines are most helpful when placed on the heart.

Moonstone

The moonstone can help bring about lucidity in dreams. Lucid dreaming means you are fully aware that you are dreaming. Lucid dreams can be really exciting, and best of all, you will be able to recall the guidance even better when you wake up. The moonstone is also a beautiful, emotional healing stone; it balances feminine and male energies and calms down feelings of stress. Like amethyst, moonstone also helps you if you have insomnia, so this is another great stone to place under your pillow if you have trouble falling asleep.

5

Messages from Your Nightmares

Oh, the terror of nightmares! Cold chills are running down your spine, and the horrifying images from the dream can haunt you for hours. Your mind is going wild, and you may even wonder why you are being punished with something so awful and terrifying as a scary nightmare.

When a cold nightmare comes around, going to bed at night can even be dreaded because of the fear that the dream will come back. It doesn't need to be that way. In contrast to the scary feelings they bring about, nightmares are here to help you heal.

The jolt you experience when waking up from a nightmare is designed to capture your attention. Perhaps there is an unhealthy situation in your life that needs to change, or maybe you are weighed down by unprocessed feelings and emotions. These types of emotional blockages could turn life-threatening if they are not resolved. The good news is that the healing path opens as soon as you acknowledge your dreams and start working with them. By connecting with your nightmares, you develop the power to transform their negative energy into something truly beautiful and loving.

THE NATURE OF NIGHTMARES

Nightmares come around when you have pushed away an issue in your life for too long. Your ordinary dreams help bring your attention to life situations that need more tender love and care. If you choose not to listen to your dreams, they come back in stronger and more dramatic form. Eventually, you will have no choice but to listen to your nightmares. Your higher self has succeeded—you are now fully aware of your dreams.

When a nightmare comes back in the same form, you now have a recurring dream. Or you may experience different nightmares every night. In those instances, your dreams are simply trying different ways of getting the message through to you.

The best approach is always to work with all your dreams. This way, you ensure that no dream needs to develop into a nightmare. With some types of dreams and life situations, it is recommended to seek professional help. This applies particularly to nightmares that have developed from a real-life trauma, also known as PTSD: Post Traumatic Stress Disorder.

TRAUMA DREAMS

You can work with trauma dreams in the same manner as you would with a "regular" nightmare. It is important to seek professional guidance and help ensure that you have all the support you need in the process. Like nightmares, trauma-related dreams occur to help you become more aware of emotions and experiences that need to be processed, accepted, and released.

If you are re-experiencing a terrifying event in your dreams that you once experienced in daily life, it is crucial to seek professional help. It is important to remember that the dream is not here to punish you or make it worse for you. The nightmare is here as your friend. It is occurring to help you realize that you still need to process the event further and that there are blocked emotions and unprocessed feelings within you. Once the emotional connection to the event's feelings has been acknowledged, the pain will not carry as much weight as it used to. You may even be able to transform the energy. When blocked emotions are released, your body, mind, and soul now have the power to heal again.

NIGHTMARES FROM THE ASTRAL PLANE

Now and then, a nightmare from the astral plane sneaks through, and those can be particularly terrifying! There are two types of astral nightmares:

1. The nightmare where an archetypal image, such as a dragon or enormous snake, has been "borrowed" from the astral plane to highlight something that is currently going on in your life.

2. The nightmare where you may experience darker energies. If you feel unbalanced and emotionally weak and have high levels of substances in your body, including alcohol, you are more susceptible to dark energy dreams.

The second type of astral nightmares that involve the presence of darker energies can be very frightening. If you have these types of dreams, the best remedy to keep these types of dark elements away from your peaceful realm is to surround yourself in white light before going to bed and staying away from recreational drugs. The combination of light and intention has the power to set you in the right vibrational frequency before drifting off to sleep. The other suggestions detailed below can be used with all types of nightmares, whether or not they were caused by a real-life trauma or "dreamed up" by your higher self to highlight an issue that needs to be addressed.

BECOME A NIGHTMARE PEACEMAKER

You can take steps to make peace with your nightmares by illuminating the issues that need to be faced, releasing blocked emotions, and processing what needs to be worked on. You can find inner peace.

Write the Dream
Give the dream your full attention. By writing down the dream, you reduce the emotional charge.

Identify the Dream Type
Nightmares are rarely intuitive, as intuitive dreams are typically not filled with emotions. If the dream, for example, is objective (see chapter 3), and you are being *chased*, ask yourself if you have experienced a similar feeling in your daily life. Most chasing dreams stop once we find a way to deal with the issue we are afraid to face in our daily life.

Make Associations
All dream symbols in your dream were chosen for a reason. A symbol can be an event, a dream figure, a location, sound, smell, etc. Write down all associations you have for each of the symbols, and see which associations "clicks" for you.

Explore / Re-enter Your Dream
Carl Jung referred to the art of reentering our dream as *Active Imagination*.[1] You can enter a dream while awake and imagine you are talking to the dream figures or the dream in general. Always surround yourself in white light before entering a dream. Ask the dream what it is trying to tell you and see what answers you get. Write down the answers. Your feelings are crying out to be acknowledged, and they will get attention in this process. Once they are acknowledged, the blockages are released, and you now have the room you need to heal.

Create a New Ending

Decide how you would like a dream to end if it ever comes back. This step will give you an immense sense of power and control, and the effects from this mind-changing reframing will reverberate throughout your daily life as well. You are now creating new solutions in your dreams, and the changes will be felt on every level of your life. By experiencing a resolution in your dream, you will also feel empowered in your daily life.

6

Synchronicity: Guidance is All Around You

We all experience coincidences. In this chapter, we are not concerned with those daily little coincidences that pass us by as soon as they happen, such as two neighbor dogs running after the ball at the same time. Instead, we're talking about the type of extraordinary coincidence that feels so surprising and remarkable that it has the power to shift your perceptions in the most powerful way imaginable.

Suppose you were asked to reflect upon some remarkable coincidences in your own life. In that case, you could probably think of at least a few occurrences that were just too extraordinary to be considered everyday incidents. Perhaps something amazing happened that reminded you of a dream, or maybe you were thinking of a friend you had not seen in years when he or she unexpectedly called you. Such events have the power to change our lives beautifully and even to fuel us with just the right amount of energy and trust to continue in a certain direction. An inner state, which could be a thought, a feeling, or a dream image, coincides with an outer event, and there is just no rational explanation for these types of occurrences. You just know that something meaningful, and something very important, is happening. You have experienced a synchronistic event!

Carl Jung originally coined the term synchronicity after he experienced some truly remarkable and meaningful coincidences himself.[1] In his definition of synchronicity, Jung was careful to differentiate synchronicity from a synchronous event with "meaning." A synchronous event can be described as anything that is happening at the same time. For example, school classes start simultaneously in different schools, but no one sees anything significant in these "coincidences." In a synchronistic event, however, the meaningful "coincidence" may well occur simultaneously, but it is rather your subjective reaction that is happening within you that brings the events together in a meaningful way.

Isn't it quite intriguing to think about how an image within you can suddenly show up in the outer world as well? Synchronistic events connect your inner and outer worlds. Even though someone next to you may see what is happening in this outer event, they cannot fully understand the significance. Only you can, as you are the only one who knows what you were thinking about at the time. Hence, you can rest assured the guidance is for you only when you are experiencing a synchronistic event!

This connection, or the unity, between our inner and outer worlds, was referred to by Jung as the *Unus Mundus*, "the potential world outside of time."[2] In the *Unus Mundus*, everything is interconnected, and there is no difference between the past, present, and future. Central to the *Unus Mundus* is the collective unconscious, the field shared by all living beings (see chapter 1). This concept forms a particularly important part of synchronicity. It can even be seen as the backbone of all synchronistic experiences since this is the connected field we tap into when we dream. This powerful field is commonly referred to as the astral plane and can also resemble the Eastern philosophy of an underlying Tao.

When we experience synchronicity, we begin to truly understand how everything around us is interconnected and how we get to tap into this power in our dream realms. Just imagine the possibilities you have every night when you go to sleep!

OUR TEACHER AND GUIDE

When synchronistic experiences come our way, they are spontaneous and unexpected. To fully appreciate synchronicities, therefore, and to even notice them, awareness is the key. If we are not conscious about what we are thinking or feeling, how could we possibly see the link to something that is also happening around us?

Becoming aware of synchronistic events can have immense significance in your growth process. You can look at symbols in synchronistic events the same way you would when you interpret dreams by asking yourself what they represent. In what way are you being guided? You can amplify the synchronistic event to see where this particular situation applies to your current life right now. A synchronistic event does not happen by chance. It has always come your way for a reason!

If you pay close attention to the symbols that showed up in your dreams before starting your day, the chances of experiencing a synchronistic event are much higher as you now are fully aware of your inner state.

EXAMPLES OF SYNCHRONICITY

A dream preceded one of the best-known synchronicities experienced by Jung and beautifully shows the interconnectedness of our inner and outer worlds and how this insight can help fuel a healing process. Jung was one day sitting in his office listening to one of his female clients sharing a dream she'd had the previous night about a golden scarab.[3] The same moment she talked about the scarab, there was a knock on the window, and when Jung turned around, he found to his astonishment that it was a beetle with a golden shine that was trying to get inside. Jung's client was so surprised that she bounced up, and the event helped her open herself up to the therapy process.

The dream of the scarab was an event in her inner psychic state, and this inner symbol was, in turn, mirrored by an outer event in the form of a beetle. A beetle may be the type of bug that looks most like a scarab, and it flew into the room just at a time when the therapy was progressing rather slowly, and Jung felt the client was stuck. We can turn to mythology for further guidance when exploring what the scarab as a symbol may represent here. In his book *Synchronicity: An Acausal Connecting Principle*, Jung discusses how the scarab is used as a symbol for rebirth in Egyptian mythology. So this synchronistic event can be seen as having helped the client become reborn, as it turned out to have such a significant and life-changing effect on the therapeutic process.[4]

The Number 137

Synchronicity events do not need to be of a major size to have a significant impact. Sometimes the smallest events can provide the most astounding guidance. The following synchronistic event happened in my own life some years back, and it beautifully inspired me to share my passion for dreams and synchronicity with more people.

A friend of mine I had just met three days earlier had given me a very interesting scientific journal to read about number archetypes and control theory. A central part of the study had to do with Wolfgang Pauli's fascination with the number 137. According to Pauli, this number is highly special. It has been found to be the sum of all constants in nature.[5] Pauli was one of the true pioneers in quantum physics. As a longtime student of Jung, I knew that Jung and Pauli had come to influence each other greatly in their respective fields, particularly concerning synchronicity. As synchronicity had always fascinated me, I was now absolutely delighted to dive into this intriguing journal. A few minutes after reading the study, I decided to watch an old movie I had not seen in many years from the cable box movie gallery. I viewed the movie, and much to my surprise and astonishment, the number 1:37 flashed up on my screen just as it finished! In this modern era with DVDs and streaming, the length of movies typically does not appear at the end, but since this was a purchased movie from the cable box, the movie length just popped up on the screen, in a large oversized font. I instantly felt very excited and inspired. I knew I was on the right track and that this was a subject I needed to study closer and share with many people immediately.

At the time, I was also part of the organizing committee for an upcoming regional conference for the International Association for the Study of Dreams. When I was asked if I would like to hold a symposium at the conference, I immediately said yes, and agreed to discuss dreams and synchronicity. The synchronistic event I had experienced filled me with such inspiration and so much energy that I knew with all my heart that this was a subject I wanted to share with the world.

These beautifully connected events illustrate how even the smallest coincidences can serve as powerful guidance and help fuel us with the energy we need, and point us in the right direction, just when we need it!

When you listen to your dreams
you make room for miracles.

* * *

A fairy once took me to fairyland,
She held my hand, and conveyed her story,
in a way that I could understand.

* * *

Dreams come true,
when you pursue them
with an open heart.

7

Intuitive Dreams

The most exciting dreams of all may be the ones that are mysteriously connected to events in the future and dreams where we tap into the life of someone else! Some dreams can be highly revealing and sometimes so filled with premonitions they even stun us. You may, for example, dream about the name of someone you have never met before, and then you meet a person with just that name the very next day. Or you may dream about the new interiors of a friend's house, only to hear the next day that they have indeed redesigned their house exactly the way you saw it in your dream. Or perhaps you dream that your friend is feeling a certain way, just to hear the next day that it's true. When you tap into someone else's feelings and thoughts or receive direct information in some way, you are having a telepathic dream.

VALUABLE GUIDANCE

In my dream-guidance sessions, I encourage my clients to pay particular attention to events in their outer life that remind them of anything they have dreamt about. Whether it may be a literal telepathic dream or a more symbolic synchronicity experience, any moments of guidance often occur at important transition points in our lives. As we saw in the earlier chapter, synchronistic events can help fuel us with the energy we need to continue in a certain direction. They may help prepare us for a future event so that we are better equipped when it happens.

Sometimes we dream about something that is happening, at the exact moment in time, in the outer world. For example, a person may be on holiday and dream about a fire in their home and then receive a phone call at that exact point in time telling them that their house is, in fact, on fire. The fact that two events located far from each other in the physical realm can happen simultaneously in our inner and outer worlds make us realize that the concepts of both time and space may not be what we think they are. Jung, along with many other prominent researchers and scientists, proposed that neither space nor time consists of anything.[1] Rather, these are concepts we have constructed to make sense of our experiences. Synchronistic and telepathic phenomena show how inner and outer events can occur simultaneously. Simultaneous or not simultaneous, the events in synchronistic and telepathic events are so deeply connected, they are not limited by time and space![2]

DREAM GUIDANCE

HOW DO WE KNOW IT'S INTUITION?

How do we know when we are receiving true guidance, when we have a telepathic dream, and which types of dreams are more oriented toward helping us process our feelings and emotions?

All types of dreams are equally important. Just because you may not be receiving messages to solve the mystery of the universe in a dream doesn't mean you are not growing. Every single dream you have helps you in one form or the other. Dreams may not always offer you premonitions, but many dreams can help you work through unconscious feelings and reactions, and the process in itself helps remove the emotional blockages that are weighing you down. Dreams also help enhance your awareness. As you clear your energy from emotional blockages, you become more receptive to receiving guidance, not only in your dreams but also in your daily life.

How do you know when you're receiving a premonition, so you can take action? While there is no definite answer to this question, if you keep a dedicated dream writing practice and carefully write down all your dreams, you may decode patterns and determine certain themes and feelings around your intuitive dreams.

As detailed earlier in this book, if you're feeling *emotionally charged* and involved in a dream, the chances are higher that the dream helps you process an emotional feeling or highlight an issue in your life that you may be unaware of.

On the other hand, if you're experiencing something in a dream without any significant feelings attached to it, and you may even feel like you're watching a movie. You may indeed be receiving intuitive guidance or experiencing a telepathic dream. Also, intuitive dreams are sometimes more "sequential" and logical, with a proper storyline developing. In contrast, emotional dreams tend to be more incoherent, but there is no clear answer. You need to trust your intuition.

In telepathic dreams, we generally tap into the feelings or life issues of someone else instead of processing our own emotions and feelings, and as a general rule of thumb, we tend to feel more like we're "a fly on the wall" in those types of dreams. We are just making a quick visit, and if we are interacting with any dream characters, the discussion can be surprising, but it doesn't usually stir up too much of an emotional reaction. Rather than feeling upset, we are taking in the information, treasuring every moment.

Concerning "taking action" after having had an intuitive dream, it needs to be noted that there is just not much we can do with some types of premonitions. We may have received an image about an upcoming event in a dream, but we often don't have enough information to make sense of it or even know when or where it will happen. Many people dreamt about the World Trade Centre attack in September 2001 during the nights and even weeks preceding the tragic event. However, even though many of the dreams involved fire, airplanes, and columns, they did not contain enough information to say where the tragedy would occur and who would be involved.

Sometimes, intuitive dreams come to us to prepare for events and make it easier to handle them as they happen. At other times, they help us pay extra attention to such events, as there may be an important value in them. There may be a major significance and link to a particular event, also in your personal life. See what is happening in your life right now and how the premonition you had may also relate to your life circumstances. Likewise, if you are having a telepathic dream about a friend's current life circumstances, ask yourself why this information has been revealed to you at this particular point in time. How do you benefit from receiving this knowledge right now?

INTUITION ENHANCEMENT

The best way of enhancing your intuition is to pay close attention to your dreams every morning and practice higher awareness daily. By keeping your dream images alive throughout the day, you become more receptive to the symbols, messages, and parallel events in your daily life.

You can also boost your intuition by asking yourself questions at night before you go to sleep. Begin with easier questions, such as what song you will hear playing on the radio the next day or who will call you first thing in the morning. With time, you can advance your questions by wishing to receive guidance about certain situations or help with major life decisions. Pay close attention to your dreams as you wake up, and look for any clues that may have been revealed to you. By processing each dream in detail (see chapter 3), the messages will start shining through, even if, at first, you may not think the dream has provided you with any guidance.

Remember, guidance comes your way when you are ready to receive it. By continuously working with your dreams, you keep enhancing your awareness levels and become even more receptive to the beautiful messages that are there for you. It truly is a win-win situation!

8

Dream Themes

The dream interpretation examples in this chapter have been chosen to help you move in the right direction as you explore your dreams to understand their meanings better. Even though your dreams are indeed uniquely personal to you in many ways, we all encounter some common dream themes from time to time. Some of those "popular types of dreams" are highlighted here, along with some good sample questions you can ask your dreams as you unveil their real message!

In contrast to the more generic guides you typically find in popular dream dictionaries, the dream interpretation approach I have developed is more intuitive in that it emphasizes the importance of your *feelings* in the dream and also assists you in establishing the context by encouraging you to ask specific *questions* about the dream. Your intuition will ultimately be the best guide as you decode the different symbols. The context, or setting, such as dreaming of a dolphin in a bathtub, may have very different meanings to you than it would for someone else, depending not only on what you felt and experienced in the dream but also on your background and the personal associations you have with both dolphins and bathtubs. A dream dictionary may, for example, tell you that a dolphin symbolizes happiness and joy and that a bathtub represents rejuvenation or "cleansing," but it will most likely fail to ask you what you associate with dolphins or bathtubs. It may also ignore that a bathtub in this situation could also be viewed as "restricting." Why is the dolphin in such a small space? Perhaps you have a unique memory of a dolphin or have always been intrigued by dolphins for some reason. Did something of significance ever happen to you in a bathtub? What does a dolphin mean to you? You are the only one who will ever know for sure what the dream meant, and it is your intuition that will help guide you more than anything else!

ANIMAL KINGDOM

Animals are symbolic characters, and just like people, they appear in our dreams for a very specific reason. Animal dreams are often very spiritual, and many native tribes believe that animals in our dreams empower us with the qualities of their spirit. They are also viewed as our guardians.

Sometimes animals are brought into your dream to help highlight parts of yourself in one form or the other. Animals also appear in intuitive and astral dreams as special messengers of important information. If you are dreaming of a pet who has passed over, it could be an astral visit.

Insights from the Animal Kingdom

What comes to mind when you think about the type of animal in your dream? *Eagles, dolphins, and elephants* are all very spiritual animals and often show up in astral dreams with specific messages and insights for us. What comes to mind when you think of elephants? For many people, elephants symbolize wealth and abundance, along with spiritual insights. Depending on your personal history and background, the associations you make with each animal in your dream will be helpful clues in the dream interpretation process.

A fascinating animal dream symbol is the *snake*. Snakes represent so many things. Naturally, they can be highly dangerous and poisonous, but they also bring wisdom and new beginnings. They shed their skin and have transformational energy. In Eastern traditions, the divine Kundalini energy dormant within us is portrayed as a snake curled up at the bottom of the spine.

If you are dreaming of a snake, on a subjective level, it could indicate that you have some snake-like qualities within you—perhaps you are more venomous to people around you than you think, but the snake may also have appeared to help you find your inner wisdom, or help you activate your inner Kundalini energy. Your feelings in the dream will help guide you to see what's going on.

On a more objective level, the dream could highlight that you feel someone in your surrounding is attacking you, and the dream could help you process the situation. Symbolic snakes are popular visitors from the astral plane and could enter your dream as an archetypal force to highlight something going on in your life or bring a unique message to you.

Astral dreams can also occur in dream states where we are half sleeping and half awake, and dream figures from the animal kingdom sometimes appear in this realm. If you "wake up" at night and see a beautiful unicorn standing next to you, listen to your heart. Messages from the animal kingdom are conveyed through feelings. A miraculous visit filled with love and light will, of course, make you feel better than a dark visit by spiders and bugs. If you attract lower energy visitors, go back to chapter 5 and learn how to surround yourself with white light before bed.

CHASING DREAMS

Many of us have been chased by a frightening being in our dream at some point. On a subjective level, a chasing dream could appear to help you see that you may be running away from something that is going on within you. Taking a more objective approach, you could be trying to get away from someone around you or a specific situation in your daily life. Nightmares of being chased are very common and help showcase how we either live in denial or don't face our fears in daily life.

Insights from Being Chased

Ask yourself what it is you may be afraid of facing. What are you running away from? Is there a side to yourself you may not see or perhaps feel uncomfortable about? Or are you trying to escape from a situation or avoiding someone in your life? Think about what it is you fear in life. By asking yourself these questions, you build up higher awareness about what is going on in your life, and you will find the strength to deal with your situation.

Chasing dreams will keep haunting you until you develop higher awareness about yourself and until you can work through and face what you are scared of. When you are being chased, it is time to take a big leap into the tiger's mouth and face your fears!

DRIVING DREAMS

How you drive your car or any other vehicle type in a dream can help you see what is happening in your life right now. How is your journey? Are you traveling through life smoothly, or are you going backward and spinning out of control in all directions?

Insights from Driving Dreams

Can you see the road in front of you, or is it all dark? Are the breaks functioning? If you're about to crash or do crash in the dream, it could be a warning sign that this is the direction in which your life is moving if you don't do anything to change things around. It could, of course, also be a reflection that something has already gone wrong in your life. What can you do to rectify the situation? Remember, when one door closes, another door opens!

If you're driving up a hill but don't have enough power to continue but instead start rolling backward, it is a good indication that this is also how you feel in your life right now. You're almost there, but you can't quite make it. Think about what happened the day before the dream, take up the context, and see how it relates to your current life circumstances. You are receiving guidance every night!

DYING IN DREAMS

Death in dreams rarely indicates that you or someone else is dying. If someone is about to die in real life, most guidance in dreams tends to be more symbolic. For instance, instead of dreaming about a relative's actual death, you may dream that they are standing next to you with a packed suitcase, symbolizing that they are "going away." A dream of an actual impending death often has more life-changing themes, such as moving to a new place or embarking on a long journey. So if you dream that you are dying, it most likely does not foretell that you are. However, it could be a good indication that it is time for you to thoroughly examine what is going on in your life. A situation as you know it may now have ended.

Insights about Dying in Dreams

If you died in the dream, ask yourself in what way a situation in your life has ended right now. Remember, new beginnings follow endings, and new doors will open! Now may be a good time for you to pause and reflect. By focusing inward, you will find your true path.

EMOTIONS IN DREAMS

Emotions in dreams are highly indicative of how you are feeling, and such dreams can be worth their weight in gold, especially in times of denial and when you are lying to yourself. As most dreams are highly subjective and try to highlight things about you, the way other people feel in your dream is often a reflection of your inner emotional state.

Insights from Emotions in Dreams

If there are *sad* people around you, this could be a sign that you are feeling sad. Take the time to heal, and remember that forgiveness is the most powerful healer. If your dream is filled with *angry* people, this could be a reflection of your own unprocessed or unresolved anger. It may be time for you to let go of past disappointments. Of course, the dream could also be objective and help you understand a relationship better by bringing about all the feelings and emotions involved.

FAIRIES IN DREAMS

Fairies sometimes visit us in dream realms and give us a sparkling touch of magic and belief! They often appear in difficult times, just as we need love and hope the most. Like visitors from the animal kingdom, fairy encounters often happen in astral dreams when we are half awake and half asleep. These types of dreams are so miraculous and special that they may even stay with us forever after.

Insights from Fairies in Dreams

What is happening in your life right now? What were you thinking about before going to sleep? There are many fascinating stories about people who have had visits from fairies in times of despair and distress and how they beautifully woke up with a magical spark of excitement and a wonderful sense of belief in miracles all around! These types of dreams can feel amazingly real, and you may also be taken on a "dream voyage" to the land of the fairies or receive a little surprise visit from a fairy in your own home.

FALLING DREAMS

When you're falling in a dream, whether in freefall or in an elevator that is heading down, this is a good indication it's time to reevaluate your life situation. Whereas going up in life is considered positive, falling downward is generally not an encouraging sign. These dreams are often warning signals, so it is important to pay close attention to what is happening.

Insights from Falling Dreams

Ask yourself where in your life you may feel like something is not going the way you planned. The solution you're seeking may be right in front of you. Remember, there is a positive in each situation, and it is important not to focus too much on the negative. What can you do to fix it? Can you redirect what is happening somehow? If it is not possible to physically do something about the situation, remember you can always change your attitude, inviting more positive thoughts into your life. By processing what's happening, you clear energetic blockages and now have the space to attract more positive thoughts.

FLYING DREAMS

Whether you're flying by yourself or in an airplane, flying in a dream brings feelings of ultimate freedom, happiness, and excitement. From a spiritual lens, dreams of flying help you see the world from a higher perspective.

Insights from Flying Dreams

Whether you are flying on your own or in an airplane, you are reaching new heights, and this may also be how you feel in daily life. Now is a great time to stretch your wings and fly! You may have underestimated your abilities, and the dream has appeared to help you develop more belief in yourself.

If you're afraid of *crashing* or do crash, this could indicate that your life is out of control in some way. Where may this be applicable? Any type of crash dream is often a warning sign that you need to change what you are currently doing, so pay close attention to such dreams!

Sometimes we spread our wings so high that we reach new realms altogether. High above the clouds, you may find a sacred land, or golden temple filled with unique wisdom, just for you, just when you need it the most. These types of celestial dreams are miraculous, and the insights gained from such journeys can be life-changing.

GARDEN DREAMS

A garden is a sacred place. This is where your creative seeds and planted and your projects come to life. If you dream of someone stealing your vegetables in the garden, this could indicate that you feel what you've been planting has been taken away from you.

Insights from Garden Dreams

As with all dreams, pay close attention to your feelings in the dream. Do you feel happy and serene spending time in your blossoming garden, or do you feel guilty because it has been deserted? What could you do to nurture your creative garden better? If the garden has been destroyed, you may have experienced a loss in your life, either on a financial level or perhaps a more spiritual, inner power level.

HAIR LOSS DREAMS

Losing your hair in a dream can be very distressing. How you feel in the dream often reveals the true story, so think about what effect the hair loss or haircut in the dream had on you. Did you feel happy and excited about the change or devastated? Hair could be associated with personality, beauty, self-confidence, power, and youth. Think about what is going on in your life right now and how these events affect you.

Insights from Hair Loss Dreams

If you're a woman and dream of losing your hair, it may be an indication that you're not feeling very feminine at the moment. Perhaps your partner has lost sexual interest. If you're a man and your hair falls off or is cut off too short, think about what may be causing you to feel this way. Maybe you lost out on a project at work, or perhaps a younger colleague got the promotion you've been working so hard for.

If you dream that your *scalp is falling off* as well, the changes you're currently experiencing may now be affecting you to the point that you are hurting. The notion that your scalp is tearing puts an extra spin on such dreams. Whatever personal associations you have with your hair, they all need your "scalp" to flourish and grow. If the scalp is not there, it means all the qualities you associate with your hair will not be able to grow back until you heal the scalp. These types of dreams could be urging you to take precautions and rectify the situation.

HOUSE DREAMS

A house in a dream is often a representation of you. It is your sacred temple! Do you feel safe in the house? Is it old or new, filled with inspiration or sadness? Remember any symbols in the dream, such as open or closed doors, floors, and also pay attention to any new rooms that you may find.

Insights from House Dreams

If you feel safe and the house is *fresh and bright,* it could signify that you feel calm and happy in your life right now. In contrast, dreaming of a *little shed* falling apart in an earthquake may indicate that you are not grounded enough and may need to focus more on your daily life on creating more security for yourself.

Doors in a dream often indicate that you have some decisions to make. If the doors are closed, it may not be quite your time yet. Think about where this may currently apply in your life. If the doors are open, the dream may show you it is time to move ahead now; you can move forward! There are no blockages, and the door is open! Open doors could also be an intuitive sign that great new opportunities are coming your way or are perhaps already present around you.

Dark houses, as well as dark dreams in general, often show a lack of awareness. You can enhance your awareness by paying more attention to your dreams and dedicating yourself to daily meditation practice.

When you stumble upon *new rooms* in a dream house or even new stores in a shopping mall, you could be finding something new about yourself. Perhaps you are not aware of your full potential and everything you are capable of. It is important to ask yourself what type of room you have found.

A *basement* could be a representation of your unconscious. Pay close attention to what is happening down there! You can learn a lot about yourself.

On the other hand, a higher floor often shows your higher self and your higher potential. Perhaps you are reaching new insights.

A *sink, bathtub, or shower* often appears in our dreams when we have done something we feel guilty or uncomfortable about or when we feel ready to "cleanse" ourselves.

LOST IN DREAMS

When you dream that you are lost, the chances are that this is also how you feel in waking life. You may be feeling confused, or maybe even meaningless inside, as though you don't know the way forward. You may have been distracted from your true path or lost connection with family and friends, and the dream has appeared to help you find your way again.

Insights from Being Lost
If you *can't find your way* or don't know where you are, think about where in your life you feel lost right now. By implementing a daily meditation practice, you can enhance your awareness and help you find inner peace and a sense of purpose and direction.

If there is *fog* in your dream, ask yourself what you may not want to see in your waking life. As with all dreams, your background, life situation, and memories will ultimately guide you as you find the true message in a dream.

Dream Themes

LOVEMAKING DREAMS

Lovemaking dreams can be so beautiful and feel amazingly real. You may not always know the person you're making love with in your dream, but as we have touched upon earlier, when we dream about other people, what our dream is trying to do on a subjective level is to show us different aspects of ourselves. In romantic dreams, the emphasis is often on our feminine and masculine aspects. As mentioned earlier in this book, in the Jungian school of psychology, our feminine and masculine qualities are anima and animus. The feminine side within a man is his anima, and the masculine side of a woman is her animus.[1] As long as our anima and animus are unconscious, we are not utilizing our full abilities, and we may even feel surprised by our unknown reactions! Lovemaking dreams are a great way of bringing these qualities into consciousness.

Insights from Lovemaking Dreams

Do you feel in balance? If you're dreaming of making love to *someone you know*, remember that the person in your dream has been chosen for a very specific reason! What comes to mind when you think about your dream lover? What do you like about him or her? On a subjective level, a lovemaking dream may be trying to tell you that you would benefit from taking on some of the qualities of that particular person. From an objective perspective, it could also be a sign that it would be good for you to work with them closer—perhaps there is a project developing on the horizon? If you are making love to an ex-partner, you may now be ready to move "beyond the hurt." Perhaps you feel ready to forgive and forget and move on with your life. It could also signify that you still love them and that you will always have a beautiful connection.

If you don't know the partner in your dream, the partner could indeed be an aspect of yourself on a subjective level. Reflect upon how your lover acted and any personality characteristics that may also be present within you. If you're a woman making love to a man, what stands out about him? He likely represents your animus, your masculine qualities. Do you see yourself in him? Could you benefit from expressing yourself more like the man in your dream? From a more objective perspective, the dream could help you feel truly loved. Treasure such dreams and keep them alive as you go about your day! When you feel happy and resonate on a higher frequency and feel as if what you wish for has already happened, that's when you begin to attract good things all around!

As with all dreams, lovemaking dreams could also be intuitive guidance dreams, in which case your dream lover may be waiting for you around the corner!

MANDALA DREAMS

A mandala is a beautiful round symbol that often contains geometrical shapes. *Mandala* is a Sanskrit word for "circle." Mandalas can sometimes appear spontaneously in our dreams or during meditations. A mandala is a very powerful dream symbol and shows up to both guide and heal you! Dreams of mandalas often come about when we are in the process of finding our true path. The circular image symbolizes healing and integration. The mandala can be seen as a beautiful circular force integrating all aspects of yourself.

Insights from Mandala Dreams

When a mandala appears, whether in a dream or during meditation, it is a sign you are finding your real calling. How can you best stay on your true path? What have you done lately that symbolizes healing and integration? If you notice yourself experiencing more inner peace from meditation and dreamwork, keep up the good work!

NAKED DREAMS

Most people have found themselves naked in a dream at some point in their lives. These types of dreams are mainly subjective and come about to highlight how we feel about ourselves. Some naked dreams can be very embarrassing, whereas others make us feel like we're giving away too much of ourselves or that people can see right through us.

Insights from Being Naked in Dreams

If you are *naked* in a dream, you may recently have revealed something embarrassing or felt exposed somehow and did not enjoy it—maybe you felt unprepared and afraid everyone saw it. It could also be a sign that you are guilty about something in your life right now. Perhaps something you have said or done? Maybe you have talked too much about yourself or someone else?

If you feel *naked and happy*, it would probably do you good if you showed more of yourself. Perhaps you would benefit from being more honest and show people who you are. As always, when you work with your dreams, think about how you felt in the dream, and the answer will come to you.

PREGNANCY / BABY

Dreaming of a new life growing within you could be a sacred message that you are pregnant or a premonition that you will be blessed with a baby soon! In other instances, these types of dreams reflect the potential for growth in your life. A new birth could be about to happen, perhaps within you.

Insights from Pregnancy / Baby Dreams
The baby developing inside you could represent some beautiful changes happening within you. The baby you are about to give birth to or have just given birth to may indeed be a new you. Are you perhaps about to transform your life in some way? Think about what projects you have going on that may be blossoming right now? If you can't think of any, this may be a very good time to develop something. Are there perhaps some new ideas cooking on the stove? Look around you and see what is happening

and use the guidance from the dream as you decide to move forward or continue in a new direction.

SCHOOL AND EXAMS

Being back in school is a popular dream, and this type of dream is often highly subjective, as it shows what is currently going on within you. When you dream that you're back in school, it is a good indication that you're not feeling prepared for something, and it's time to brush up your knowledge a bit.

Insights from School and Exam Dreams
If you suddenly find yourself taking an *exam* you haven't studied for; you're probably feeling overwhelmed or simply unprepared in daily life. You may have an important meeting coming up that you don't feel ready for. Take a good look at your situation and see what you can do to acquire the knowledge you need to feel better equipped and more confident that you are indeed good enough and know enough!

STUCK OR POWERLESS IN DREAMS

Being stuck or feeling powerless in a dream often reflects that you wish your life were different somehow, but you feel unable to do something about it. You may be struggling with a decision or feel the need to move on. Trust your intuition and move forward!

Insights from Being Stuck or Powerless in Dreams
Where do you feel stuck right now? Around what issues do you have conflicting emotions? What can you do to free yourself and get your power back? Can you perhaps develop a new attitude? Your inward search for answers will reward you. Think about what aspects of your life you can change.

TEETH DREAMS

Dreams about your teeth can have multiple meanings. Your teeth are used to chew and process your food, and teeth-themed dreams could symbolize your ability to process challenges and the way you view your power. Because teeth are located in your mouth, they also relate to the way you communicate. False teeth could, for example, symbolize lies.

Insights from Teeth Dreams
If you're dreaming of your teeth falling out, ask yourself if you feel like you've lost your power? Always take up the context of the dream. What happened in the days before the dream? A dream about your teeth falling out could come about if you feel you have talked about something too much or said something you regret.

It is not uncommon for these types of dreams to occur when we feel insecure and unable to handle life's challenges—that is, we can't "chew on" events. As with all dreams, consider how you feel in the dream to determine best how this dream relates to your daily life.

TRAIN DREAMS

You may be about to embark on an important journey in your life. Train dreams are often very symbolic. Unlike many other types of traveling dreams, trains are different in that they follow a set schedule and even have a specific destination.

Insights from Train Dreams

If you are running toward a train, you may feel like you're about to miss out on an important opportunity in your waking life. If you jump on the train too fast, without bringing your luggage, it may indicate that you are rushing in life and will end up wasting time because you now have to go back again and get what you forgot. Pay close attention to your feelings in the dream.

UNFAITHFUL DREAMS

If you dream that your partner is having an affair, take a deep breath. They may not be. If you feel highly emotionally charged in the dream, it will do you better if you give them the benefit of the doubt. In those instances, it is most likely an objective emotional processing dream, which is designed to help you work through a certain life situation or emotion. On a subjective level, it could even be you who is being unfaithful to yourself.

Insights from Unfaithful Dreams

If you have no reason to suspect that you are being wronged, think about what may be causing you to feel that your partner is not honest with you. From a subjective perspective, it could be you who is not being honest with yourself. Perhaps there is something you need to learn about yourself, which is being shown to you through your partner's dream actions. You may be feeling empty inside and seek more meaning and rewards. You may even be yearning to leave some aspects of your life behind, and it is now time to fill any voids in your life in healthy ways.

On the other hand, if you dreamt about the affair without feeling upset and perhaps even felt like you were watching a movie without having any emotional reaction, it could indicate that you are being guided to see what is going on around you.

WATER DREAMS

Water in dreams is sometimes a reflection of the deep unconscious part of you, and it can also represent your emotions. If the water is calm and clear, this is likely also how you feel in your daily life—you feel happy and have clarity. In contrast, if the water is dark, you may be experiencing sadness and confusion.

Insights from Water Dreams

What is the color of the water? Is it dark or light? Are the waves high, and are they crashing over you? Maybe you are experiencing a very difficult situation in life, and the dream is here to bring more awareness of your situation.

Sitting on the beach, gazing out over a beautiful pink ocean with magical fairy sparks all over, will naturally feel very different from being lost at sea! Your feelings in the dream will help serve as beautiful road signs as you find the true answers you are looking for.

With higher awareness,
　　everything feels lighter,
　　　　and here I find the answer.

9
Dreaming of Numbers

The Universe is organized by numbers. Elegant numerical equations and number sequences show up everywhere around us—in our birthdays, in our names, in house numbers, on buildings, in astronomy, in nature, and of course—in our dreams.

Numbers can provide us with magnificent guidance and insights. Over the ages, philosophers, alchemists, and scientists have turned to numbers in their quest to find answers to the deepest mysteries of the universe. The Greek philosopher and mathematician Pythagoras, who lived about 500 B.C, shared this universal quest and spent many of his years studying the fine nature of numbers. Sacred number teachings can also be found in the Jewish Kabbalah and the Chinese I Ching.

Pythagoras, who is perhaps most known for his remarkable contributions to the study of geometry, held the esoteric view that numbers were the underlying principles of all sciences. He believed that the greater knowledge of the origin of all things could be gained by a deeper understanding of numbers.[1]

Pythagoras founded an academic school where students were instructed in mathematics, music, and astronomy—the three areas Pythagoras thought of as the foundation in life. The students were taught that numbers represent a living frequency and how numbers could best be understood from a qualitative perspective.[2]

NUMBER DREAMS

Numbers show up in our dreams as sacred messengers, and it is in our highest interest to pay attention to the fine structure that so eloquently connects our waking and dreaming states. Numbers are part of an ancient Universal language, and number dreams are best understood when we look at the unique frequencies of the numbers.

In this section, you will learn how to understand your own number dreams better. As always, your dreams are unique to you, and a certain number sequence could be delivering a message that relates specifically to your life situation right now. Numbers vibrate with a divine frequency, and there could be a very special message waiting for you. The best way to find the true meaning of a number dream is to meditate on the answer.

In Pythagorean numerology, numbers are added together and then reduced to a single digit. As an illustration, 12 becomes 3 (1+2), 129 becomes 3 (1+2+9 = 12; 1+2 = 3). Master numbers 11, 22, 33, and 44 are normally not reduced further. It is important to remember that the base number behind a master number still carries a vibration, so I recommend looking at both the master number and the reduced number. It's helpful writing these numbers as 11/2, 22/4, 33/6, and 44/8.

DREAM EXAMPLE:
In your dream, you see the number 114 written on a piece of paper.

The numbers in the dream could be viewed as a date, number sequence, or individual numbers. Let's begin with reducing the numbers to a single digit.

$$1 \quad 14$$
$$1 \quad 5\,(1+4) \quad = 6$$

Here we see that the number 6 is the underlying vibration of our dream number. In the section below, you can learn more about the qualities of number 6. Number 6 vibrates with family energy, responsibility, harmony, and service.

Ask yourself how this number relates to your life right now. If this number shows up in your dream in response to a dream incubation for guidance around a particular life decision—does the harmonious family vibration of 6 help illuminate the situation? Or could there be a message for you to act more responsibly?

We could also look at each number in the sequence individually. This can be done with any numbers that appear in a dream. In this particular sequence, we have two number 1s and one number 4. We begin with number 1. The first number in a dream number always sequence carries most of the energy.

Number 1 vibrates with leader energy and could signify achievement opportunities. Where in your life could this apply right now?

The two 1s next to each other could also be read as master number 11. Number 11 radiates with divine light. This number illuminates the truth. It is a highly intuitive master number and often signifies new beginnings.

Number 4 vibrates with the energy of organization, fine order, diligent work, and financial security. When this number shows up, we know that persistence and focus will help bring results. Is there a message in your dream to be more organized and focused?

This dream illustration above shows how we can look at the numbers to better understand the underlying message. With any dream numbers, you can either reduce them to a single digit or look at them individually to see if their specific vibrations resonate with you. All numbers ultimately reduce to a number between 1 and 9. Below you will find a summary of the vibrational qualities of the first nine numbers. You will also find a description of the master numbers. Finally, I have included number 1111 as this is a number that not only frequently shows up in our dreams but is also a number that often appears in our daily life.

Dreaming of Numbers

VIBRATIONAL QUALITIES OF NUMBER 1 TO 9

1

It's time to achieve!

Number 1 reminds you of your natural leadership qualities.

When your embrace your inner self-worth and value your independence, your creativity blossoms, and you can accomplish anything.

Message: Love yourself and focus your creativity on areas where you would like to see success.

2

It is a beautiful time for making peace—
with yourself and with people around you!

Number 2 often comes into your dream to help you reflect upon how you connect with others.

This number also helps illuminate your inner sensitivity and brings a deeper understanding of other people's feelings.

Message: Nurture harmonious connections, and make a conscious decision to connect with people with an open heart.

3

Your creativity is flourishing!

Number 3 radiates with enchanting energies and often shows up to help you express your ever-flowing creativity. With number 3 in your dream, there is a good chance you now have the energy to start and complete new projects.

This number helps you find new inventive ways of creating and manifesting your dreams.

Message: This is your time to dream big and create something graceful and delightful.

4

It is time to get organized and focused!

The most structured of all numbers, when number 4 shows up in your dream, you can rest assured you would benefit from a more diligent mindset.

This number often shows up to help you see it's time to declutter your environment so that you can plan your day more efficiently.

Message: With persistence, you will achieve magnificent results. You are helped and guided!

5
Change is in the air!

When number 5 flows into your dream, there is great movement. Perhaps there are intrepid adventures over the horizon. Or maybe there are even bigger life changes unfolding.

Number 5 vibrates with the energy of fun times but is above all a number of freedom and change.

Message: This is an exciting time! Remember to stay aligned with your soul to make sure you choose changes for your highest good.

6
It is family time!

Number 6 is a number of family, responsibility, and love. When this number comes around, it could indicate that you feel responsible for other people right now.

Number 6 is a very loving energy frequency and is often associated with motherly or fatherly love and care.

It also represents harmony, structure, and balance and is expressed in nature as the six-sided hexagon.

Message: When you focus on others, you grow and expand. You are loved and protected in all that you do.

7
Look for wisdom within!

Number 7 vibrates with universal intelligence, higher wisdom, spiritual understanding, and mysticism. When 7 shows up, it's time to flow with the Divine. By staying aligned with your soul, you can master anything you wish to learn. It is a very intuitive number, and it could carry great messages for you.

Message: This is a great time to study, write, and research something that has always fascinated you. It is also a time for inner reflection and deep meditation.

8
Your dreams are coming true!

Number 8 is known as the master manifestation number. When it flows into your dreams, it could signify infinite potential for dream fulfillment.

It also comes as a reminder to stay in the light and offer guidance to those in need.

Whatever you focus on, that's the direction you're heading, so be careful what you wish for.

Message: Number 8 is a reminder to keep your focus on what you *do* want.

Dreaming of Numbers

9

Your loving generosity is flowing!

Number 9 is compassionate and humanitarian.

This number reminds you that you have the support of the entire Universe to help all of humanity and the wellbeing of the planet.

The Universe is supporting you in your growth and in your quest to help others.

Message: Being of service is a gift from heaven.

MASTER NUMBERS 11, 22, 33 & 44

Master numbers have a particularly powerful vibration. When master numbers appear, we are presented with a choice: To go high or go low. To elevate yourself to the higher end of the spectrum, you must first remember your inner soul connection. Expanding into the frequency of your souls' home in a sacred meditation will help you choose the best path forward as you discern the message from the master number.

11

Listen closely!

Number 11 vibrates with divine light and illuminates universal truth.

Pay close attention to your intuition and synchronicities when this number comes around.

Message: You are receiving a divine message
from your angels and spirit guides.

22

Manifestation time!

Number 22 is a powerful manifestation number.

When 22 comes into your life, it helps you stay focused and focus on what you want.

Message: To manifest results aligned with your soul dream, meditate before taking action.

33

Unconditional love!

Number 33 radiates with universal love.

This number flows into your life to remind you that love magnifies through forgiveness and unconditional loving service to others.

Message: You are a being of light and love.
You are loved unconditionally.

44

True fulfillment!

Number 44 reminds you that self-discipline and perseverance bring the greatest fulfillment of all.

When this number comes around, you are blessed with a true sense of achievement and abundance.

Message: By staying disciplined, you have the power to manifest wealth, abundance, and true fulfillment.

THE NUMBER SEQUENCE 1111

The Universe communicates with symbols and numbers, and certain sequences act as portals to a higher vibrational frequency. One of these sacred number sequences is 1111. This number vibrates with a divine frequency, and the moment it shows up in your life, you are receiving a special message. Think about what you were doing—in your dream or daily life—when this number showed up. What were you thinking the moment before it appeared? The message is often in the energy surrounding the number. When this number shows up in your life, you know you are guided and on your path.

The appearance of number 1111 could also be an invitation to a higher vibration. Meditating upon this number just before going to sleep is a very powerful practice and can help you align yourself with your soul's home and experience oneness with the Universe.

The study of numbers is probably the most fascinating and intriguing of all sciences. There are many great books written about the ancient science of numerology. If you are interested in studying numbers and letters in more details, I warmly recommend *The Big Book of Numerology*[3] by Shirley Blackwell Lawrence and *The Ultimate Guide to Numerology* by Tania Gabrielle.[4]

A great story in all its glory,
    is born in the heart of a dreamer.

10

Dreamy Miracles

Dreams illuminate our lives. In this book so far, we have seen how we are receiving beautiful guidance and special messages while sleeping and how the guidance is all around us also in our waking lives. The interconnectedness between our inner and outer worlds is truly astonishing. There is so much more going on both within and around us than first meets the eyes, and our dream world shows how life is not always what it seems. For example, if time and space were set in stone, how could we possibly have a dream about a person we haven't seen in years and then receive an important phone call from them the next day? Or how could we dream about something that is happening at that very moment, somewhere far away in another part of the world? Synchronistic experiences and prophetic dreams help show us that our inner and outer worlds are strongly connected. When we are being guided, we tap into something much larger than ourselves, and concepts such as time and space just seem to disappear.

You can enhance your intuition every day just by paying attention to your dreams in the morning. By keeping your dream energies alive throughout the day, you become even more open to related messages and symbols around you. Your dream images may not always be followed by exact parallel images in the outer world. Rather, *symbolic versions of a dream image* are more likely to show up in your external life. You may see something on a TV news channel, a book in a bookstore, or a specific person that reminds you of something from your dream. Pay particular attention to those moments. You are being guided for a reason! Often the meaning is not clear in the dream itself, and it is not revealed until later. Keeping careful track of your dreams in a dedicated dream journal will make it much easier for you to spot these moments as they happen. With dreamwork and higher awareness, you receive the beautiful guidance and energy you need to take you to the next place, and you now open the way for true miracles to come through.

ALL ABOUT POLARITY!

Have you ever thought about how life can be seen as being built on opposites? Think about it! We are either on the lower or higher end of any spectrum or somewhere in between. In the ancient text *The Kybalion*, which outlines basic hermetic teachings, the legendary sage Hermes

Trismegistus discusses that life is all about polarities and opposites and states that everything is dual.[1]

If we look at life from a perspective of polarities, everything can be seen as having two sides. There is just more or less of something, with manifold degrees between the two extremes. You can consciously choose to vibrate at either end of the spectrum. But if you are weighed down with blockages and negative energy patterns, it will be hard to remain on the higher end. Again, we see the true beauty of working with our dreams and clearing out negative influences to ensure we clear the space for positive affirmations and manifestations! Without blockages in the way, you are free to move around the spectrum of polarities as you wish, and you are now in a much better place. You are consciously creating rather than reacting to live events and being pushed up and down the pole.

CONFLICT RESOLUTION

How can we stay open to miracles and helpful guides if we are constantly overwhelmed by conflicts? Trust, and let go! When we trust in a good outcome, the law of opposites helps bring about a solution that matches our belief somewhere along the spectrum of polarities. The best part of letting go is that, by doing so, our conscious self is no longer the key player in the outcome, but rather our higher self (which has access to all aspects of ourselves, as well as the vast field shared by us all—the collective unconscious) now takes over and creates a new solution for us. The new and powerful answer is often presented to us in a dream or through a meaningful symbolic coincidence in our outer world, as synchronicity. So, next time you are in doubt about something or have to make a difficult decision, trust in a good outcome and let it be for a while. The best way to create a miraculous solution is to sleep on it and let your higher self guide the way.

By paying more attention to your dreams, you begin tapping into the magnificent dream field on a higher vibrational level, and this is how the flow opens up for beautiful miracles in your life. Dream analysis helps you let go of negative energy and self-destructive thought patterns and create much more space for positive thoughts when removing those negative blockages.

You now have more room to create, affirm, and manifest the life you desire, and you also become more open to miracles as they come your way. Every time you pay attention to a dream, you develop higher awareness, which will help you understand your dreams even better.

Trust is the key to manifesting a new direction in life or affirming something beautiful to happen. The well-known spiritual text *A Course in Miracles* talks about how those that trust in the outcome can wait without anxiety.[2]

The truth is that you already have the power within you to create the life you truly desire. More important than anything is the ability to trust and let go of negative anxiety. Assume the feeling that what you wish for has already happened, and you're now not only where you need to be but also where you want to be. Feel as though what you wish for has already happened and is now true. Dreams help us miraculously in the affirmation process by removing negative blockages, and even more so by making us receptive to guidance and opening room for more positive thought-forms to take place.

WISH-FULFILLMENT DREAMS PREPARE FOR MIRACLES

In addition to being filled with beautiful guidance and uniquely specific messages, dreams also help prepare you for new events coming your way. If you have a wish-fulfillment dream, make the most of that dream as you wake up! Remember and experience with your whole body, mind, and soul what it felt like to have that wish come true in your dream, and create an affirmation that resonates with this feeling. Let's say you dreamt of moving into your dream house. As you wake up in the morning, resume that feeling all over and let your happiness reverberate everywhere around and inside you. Write down a positive affirmation, such as:

> *I have found my dream home, and*
> *I resonate with gratitude and love.*

You can use the messages from your dreams to create powerful and positive affirmations for your life. Best of all, by paying more attention to the guidance you receive, your dreams will become even more unique and powerful and will help you understand the power of holding your thoughts on a positive frequency.

One night I had a beautiful dream in which I could change whatever I touched into whatever I wished for. In my dream, I even created a whole new street and changed the color of the sky!

This is a great example of the creative power we have within us. Whenever you have a positive wish-fulfillment dream, I recommend tapping into the feeling of that dream as you prepare for beautiful new events in your life. By taking on the feeling that what you wish for has already happened, you enter a much higher vibrational state, and you are now more receptive to guidance and miracles as they come your way.

Here are some examples of miraculous dream affirmations, all inspired by the magnificent dream realms:

> Anything I see and experience, I can change;
> I see what I believe.

*

> I am flying safely in higher dimensions, and I
> float in the air like a ship on the water.

*

> In my dreams, I tap into loving wisdom,
> and I receive guidance.

*

I choose positive thoughts.

*

The Wise Old Man has invited me to higher realms;
I am here now.

*

I create and direct my own life.

*

I am vibrating on higher frequency levels.

*

I am abundant in every aspect of my life, and
I happily share my gifts.

*

I am love.

Remember our earlier point about time and space? Whenever in doubt about something in your life, there is nothing more powerful than to remind yourself that everything is not really what it seems. You have the wonderful ability to shape many events around you, and what better place to receive the guidance you need to do so than from your dreams? Make use of all the beautiful messages coming your way, and start creating the life you desire.

Dreams provide us with so much wisdom. I hope this book has inspired you to go a bit deeper as you embark on your inner journey and create your own dream life.

As you ask your dreams for guidance, remember that you may sometimes receive answers that go well beyond your original question. Because your higher self is connected to the collective unconscious, dreams have the power of bringing about pretty much anything that has ever been of significance in the life of humanity.

When you are ready to receive a message, guidance, or premonition, you will. So get ready to connect with an infinite field of wisdom tonight and let your dreams lead the way. When you honor your dreams, you create the room for your soul dream to unfold, and you begin to blossom into the most loving expression of your inner magnificence.

Sweet Dreams!

Anna-Karin Björklund

*

Dream Big

Hope for the Best

Expect a Miracle!

*

Biographical Notes

PREFACE
[1] Jung, C.G. (1960). *Synchronicity: An Acausal Connecting Principle.* New York: NJ: Bollingen Foundation.

INTRODUCTION
[1] Jung, C.G. (1974). *Dreams.* Princeton, NJ: Princeton University Press.
[2] Moss, R. (2005). *Dreamways of the Iroquois: Honoring the Secret Wishes of the Soul.* Rochester, Vermont: Destiny Books.
[3] Bulkeley K. (2008) Dreaming in the World's Religions, New York, NY: New York University Press.
[4] Rinpoche, T.W. (1998) The Tibetan Yogas of Dreams and Sleep, Ithaca, NY: Snow Lion.
[5] Von Franz, M-L. (1985). *Dreams: A Study of the Dreams of Jung, Descartes, Socrates, and Other Historical Figures.* Boston, MA: Shambhala Publications, Inc.

CHAPTER 1
[1] Weitz, L. (1976). Jung's and Freud's Contributions to Dream Interpretation: A Comparison. *American Journal of Psychotherapy,* 30(2), 289. Retrieved from: http://search.ebscohost.com/login.aspx?direct=true&db=pbh&AN=5352989&site=ehost-live.
[2] Jung C.G (1959). *The Archetypes and the Collective Unconscious.* New York, N.Y: Princeton University Press.
[3] Ibid.
[4] Jung C.G. (1974). *Dreams.* Princeton, NJ: Princeton University Press.
[5] Jung C.G. (1959). *The Archetypes and the Collective Unconscious.* New York, N.Y: Princeton University Press.
[6] Ibid.
[7] Ibid.
[8] Jung C.G. (1966). *The Practice of Psychotherapy: Essays on the Psychology of the Transference and Other Subjects.* New York, N.Y: Princeton University Press.

9. Ibid.
10. Jung, C.G. (1963). *Memories, Dreams, Reflections*. New York, NY: Random House.

CHAPTER 2

1. Jung C.G. (1966). *The Practice of Psychotherapy.* New York, N.Y: Princeton University Press.
2. Ibid.
3. Jung C.G (1959). *The Archetypes and the Collective Unconscious.* New York, N.Y: Princeton University Press.

CHAPTER 3

1. Jung C.G. (1974). *Dreams.* Princeton, NJ: Princeton University Press.
2. Ibid.

CHAPTER 4

1. Naiman, R. (2017). Dreamless: The silence epidemic of REM sleep loss. Annals of the New York Academy of Sciences.

CHAPTER 5

1. Johnson, R.A. (1986). *Inner Work: Using Dreams and Active Imagination for Personal Growth.* New York, NY. Harper Collins.

CHAPTER 6

1. Jung, C.G. (1960). *Synchronicity: An Acausal Connecting Principle.* New York: NJ: Bollingen Foundation.
2. Jung, C.G. (1963). *Memories, Dreams, Reflections*. New York, NY: Random House.
3. Jung, C.G. (1960). *Synchronicity: An Acausal Connecting Principle.* New York: NJ: Bollingen Foundation.
4. Ibid.
5. Varlaki, P. (2008). Number Archetypes and "Background" Control Theory Concerning the Fine Structure Constant. *Acta Polytechnica Hungarica.* 5 (2).

CHAPTER 7

1. Jung, C.G. (1960). *Synchronicity: An Acausal Connecting Principle.* New York: NJ: Bollingen Foundation.
2. Ibid.

CHAPTER 8

[1] Jung C.G (1959). *The Archetypes and the Collective Unconscious.* New York, N.Y: Princeton University Press.

CHAPTER 9

[1] Blackwell Lawrence S. (2001/2019). *The Big Book of Numerology: The Hidden Meaning of Numbers and Letters.* Newburyport: MA: Red Wheel/Weiser.
[2] Ibid.
[3] Ibid.
[4] Gabrielle, T. (2018). *The Ultimate Guide to Numerology.* Beverly, MA: Fair Winds Press.

CHAPTER 10

[1] Three Initiates (2008). *The Kybalion: A Study of the Hermetic Philosophy of Ancient Egypt and Greece.* New York, NY: P. Tarcher/Penguin.
[2] Foundation for Inner Peace (1992). *A Course in Miracles,* Temecula, CA: Foundation for Inner Peace.

About the Author

Anna-Karin Björklund, M.A., is past board chair for the International Association for the Study of Dreams (IASD). A lifelong dreamer, she leads workshops and speaks on a luminous range of topics related to inner dream journeys and transformational soul growth. In 2007, Anna-Karin spent a month in India to deepen her meditation practice and inner connection, and her love for helping people to live an inspired life filled with love and gratitude shines through in all of her work. Anna-Karin is also a certified yoga teacher, RYT-500, and a certified reiki master teacher. She is the author of three books, including *Dream Guidance*, *Dream and Believe* and *The Dream Alchemist*.

She has been featured on NBC, CBS, FOX, and in magazines such as *Yours*, *Orange Coast*, *Marie Claire*, *Money*, and *goop*. She holds a master's degree in counseling psychology from Argosy University in Orange, California, and a bachelor's degree in tourism management from the University of Technology Sydney, Australia. Originally from Sweden, her home is now in Southern California, where she lives with her daughter and their bi-lingual French Bulldog.

Learn more at
AnnaKarinBjorklund.com

www.ingramcontent.com/pod-product-compliance
Lightning Source LLC
Chambersburg PA
CBHW031648040426
42453CB00006B/245